KU-033-564

SUMMERS WILL NEVER BE THE SAME

SUMMERS WILL NEVER BE THE SAME

A TRIBUTE TO BRIAN JOHNSTON

Edited by Christopher Martin-Jenkins & Pat Gibson

PARTRIDGE PRESS

LONDON • NEW YORK • TORONTO • SYDNEY • AUCKLAND

TRANSWORLD PUBLISHERS LTD
61–63 Uxbridge Road, London W5 5SA

TRANSWORLD PUBLISHERS (AUSTRALIA) PTY LTD
15–25 Helles Avenue, Moorebank, NSW 2170

TRANSWORLD PUBLISHERS (NZ) LTD
3 William Pickering Drive, Albany, Auckland

Published 1994 by Partridge Press
a division of Transworld Publishers Ltd

Reprinted 1994 (twice)

Copyright © In the compilation Christopher Martin-Jenkins and Pat Gibson © 1994
In his own original contribution Christopher Martin-Jenkins © 1994

The right of Christopher Martin-Jenkins and Pat Gibson to be identified
as authors of this work has been asserted in accordance with sections
77 and 78 of the Copyright Designs and Patents Act 1988.

The publishers have made every effort to contact the owners of illustrations
used in this book. Where they have been unsuccessful, they invite copyright holders
to contact them direct.

A catalogue record for this book is available from the British Library.

ISBN 185225 2324

This book is sold subject to the Standard Conditions of Sale
of Net Books and may not be resold in the U.K. below the net
price fixed by the publishers for the book.

All rights reserved. No part of this publication may
be reproduced, stored in a retrieval system, or
transmitted in any form or by any means,
electronic, mechanical, photocopying, recording,
or otherwise, without the prior permission of
the publishers.

Typeset in 10½/14pt Joanna by
Chippendale Type Ltd, Otley, West Yorkshire.

Printed and bound in Great Britain by
Mackays of Chatham PLC, Chatham, Kent

CONTENTS

'AGGERS, FREDDERS, BLOWERS ..... WHO THE HELL IS SUMMERS?!'

Geoff Thompson/Independent Newspapers

INTRODUCTION

Christopher Martin-Jenkins

Brian Johnston's gift, the best that any soul could have, was happiness. He felt it and he spread it all through his life and wherever he went. His life had its moments of sadness, disappointment and difficulty, of course, but his natural gaiety could never be repressed for long and when he came into a room, even on to the airwaves, a light came on. Enjoyment and good cheer were in the air.

This bonhomie had none of the glib glitter of some of those Show Biz personalities who are liable to tantrums or depression the moment the curtain comes down. Nor did his innate charm have any of that superficial suavity of the type adopted by some politicians. He was simply a born entertainer, in private and in public. Life was fun for him and he liked making it fun for everyone.

This book is a celebration of his wonderfully varied life and career. It has been compiled whilst the bloom is fresh. In fact it was never anything else. Until his quite unexpected heart attack at the end of November 1993, Brian – or 'Johnners' as he popularly became known, so popularly that newspaper editorials could call him that without feeling the slightest need to qualify the name – was, at eighty-one, maintaining the life of a forty-year-old with the spirit of a thirty-year-old. After a full season of BBC Radio 3 commentaries on the England versus Australia Test matches, he had done nine strenuous and brilliantly successful one-man stage shows, amusing his audiences for two hours with reminiscences and stories both tall and true. He told them in that characteristic bubbly voice at a rapid pace which gave little time for reflection.

Thus, perhaps, did he get away with the corny puns in which he so revelled. Certainly he had a way of making people laugh with a quick play on words which coming from anyone else would have sounded feeble. He had his own names for cricketers which made them, like his fellow commentators, part of the club of which *Test Match Special* listeners were also, automatically, honorary members. When Phil Newport got into the England side, he immediately became 'Pagnell' or 'Paggers'. Javed Miandad became 'Mum and I'. A man who preferred to call Ian Botham 'Bothers' or Graham Gooch 'Goochie' was bound to abbreviate Samarasekera of Sri Lanka to 'Sam' and Venkataraghavan never had much chance of being called anything but 'Old Venkers'. And so on.

On stage, or speaking after a meal, speed of delivery and joviality were the hallmarks. 'When you get to my age', he was wont to say in recent years, 'three things happen. First the memory starts to go, then . . . I'm afraid I can't remember the other two.' I don't know if it was originally his own joke, but he made it so, and he was, of course, as a personality very much an original.

His catchphrases and habits were legendary: The imitation hunting horn when greeting someone from afar. The immediate bestowal of a nickname or abbreviation upon any new acquaintance. The prompt 'How wise not to attempt the accent' whenever anyone imitated a dialect. The brown and white co-respondent's shoes worn for Test matches along with the *Test Match Special* tie – on the first day – 'to bring England luck'. The request, whenever he ordered lettuce and cucumber, for 'honeymoon salad' – followed by the explanation to a bemused – and subsequently amused – waitress of 'no dressing thank you, dear.' And so on, and so on. Such things might have turned some people into a bore. With Brian they were a constant source of amusement and endearment.

It was the way he did it, just as it was the way he told his stories.

The moment they were out he was on to the next one, mind and tongue in easy alliance. He could easily have been, indeed, either a comedian or a politician. But he was neither. He was unique: Brian Johnston the commentator, broadcaster, author, after-dinner speaker. The family man, gentleman, soldier. The eternal schoolboy. The British institution. The old-fashioned, staunchly and stubbornly conservative upholder of traditions. The stickler for punctuality and civility. The lover of all things English.

Thirty-two years my senior, he was nevertheless one of my greatest friends. I first met him in 1962 when at the suggestion of Jimmy Whatman, a mutual friend of Brian's and my father's, I went to see him whilst still at school at Marlborough. My chief memory of that occasion, like so many in which he was involved, is simply that it was great fun. He shared an office at Broadcasting House in Portland Place with another well-known television personality, Raymond Baxter, and the main decorations on the walls were a collection of those gaudy seaside postcards, whose crude but not offensive schoolboy humour always delighted him.

We had lunch at the BBC Club, now the Langham Hotel, where he made a shy schoolboy very much at ease and told me that if I wanted to be a cricket commentator I should keep playing and start practising commentaries into a tape recorder, far removed from any other spectators so as not to embarrass them or anyone else. When we next met properly I had been taken on by the BBC's sports news department after a stint with *The Cricketer*, and in the winter of 1971/72, when England had no tour, we worked together for the first time on a 'computer Test match' between the best teams from various areas of England and Australia. It was great fun for everyone, especially the tyro.

During my first 'official' commentary at the end of the 1972 season Brian again went out of his way to make me feel at home. I had dinner with him, John Woodcock and Jack Fingleton at the Swan Hotel in Bucklow Hill before the match, the first one-day international staged in England, at Old Trafford. Throughout the meal he teased 'Fingo' about the fusereum disease which had enabled Derek Underwood to undermine the Australians at the recent Headingley Test, which Fingo believed to be a conspiracy. Not that Fingo lacked a sense of humour: it was he who instantly responded with 'I beg your pardon,' when Brian pointed out Neil Harvey to TV viewers 'standing there at leg-slip with his legs apart, no doubt waiting for a tickle.' B.J. delighted in such gaffes and shamelessly traded on them. He was a broadcasting professional with an amateur's spirit.

Brian gave me a lift back to London in his yellow Ford after that match and left me in no doubt that, in his view, I had passed my first examination in the box. Thanks largely to him it had not seemed like a trial at all and I have heard many other commentators and summarizers say the same about their first experiences. From the following season, when I took over his duties as cricket correspondent after his so-called retirement from the BBC, he commentated on every home Test until the end of 1993 and I either reported or commentated on them too.

Once we reduced each other to hopeless, and helpless, giggles, on the air, when I pointed out to him that Canada's twelfth man, Showkat Baksh by name, had just come on to the field. Brian had had difficulty all morning identifying one obscure member of the polyglot Canadian team from another. The arrival of yet another, with a name he thought I had made up, was too much for him. Once Brian got the giggles, they were contagious.

A large part of my good fortune in these years was the companionship, in commentary boxes, at dinner tables and sometimes at his home in St John's Wood where there was 'always a bed when you need it' of the peerless 'Johnners'. He and Pauline were always marvellously homely hosts and my wife, Judy, and I shared holidays with them in Greece and, as so-called entertainers, on the SS *Canberra*.

This book is an attempt to recapture and pay tribute to Brian's charm, generosity and *joie de vivre* and I hope, like everything connected with him, that it will be enjoyed.

Goodness, how we will miss him in the box this summer and beyond. Especially at Lord's. I suppose it is there that I shall remember him. He was always there before me at the start of every game, an instant tonic when one arrived already tired after wrestling with heavy traffic. He would be dressed, almost always, in a smart linen suit, usually light brown in colour, but as often as not his jacket would already be off and he would be reading through his multifarious collection of listeners' letters, sleeves rolled up to reveal a pair of brawny brown arms with the tattoos which were legacies of his enterprising earlier broadcasting days and which always looked a trifle incongruous on the arms of an Old Etonian. But this was no ordinary Etonian; no ordinary Englishman.

Test match commentaries will not be the same without him; that is obvious enough. Nor were they when the wholly different, yet equally unique, John Arlott died. That is not to say, I hope, that they will not remain entertaining and informative; occasionally, perhaps, even wise. In any case, Brian's voice will forever be fresh in the BBC archives and his spirit, along with his message that cricket, like life, was a gift to be cherished, will live on.

1

THE EARLY DAYS

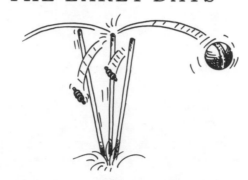

Major Christopher Johnston

Brian Johnston was the youngest of four children of a city merchant, who worked in the family coffee business in London and was also a director of the Midland Bank, and grandson of a former Governor of the Bank of England.

His elder brother, Major Christopher Johnston, who was in the 14/20 Hussars from 1932 until 1947 before farming in Herefordshire and finally settling in Berkshire where he kept livestock and indulged his passion for antiques, recalls their childhood.

Brian was born in June 1912, the year in which the family moved from the Old Rectory, Little Berkhamsted, to Little Offley, both in Hertfordshire. I suppose that it was in about 1914, being myself then four, that I first became aware of him as a person and a brother.

Little Offley was a beautiful home, a lovely old house of Tudor origins and with a Queen Anne frontage. Here, in spite of the war, we had an idyllic childhood. Lovely grounds, rolling acres over which we roamed, and large farm buildings in which we spent much time seeing the cattle and calves in their yards. We knew them all and they were part of our lives.

During the war, although living amidst plenty, my mother insisted that we took part in the rationing process and I can remember the counting of meat coupons and that awful maize bread and maize pudding, both of which we heartily disliked.

Although there was a large kitchen garden, we used to use dandelions for lettuce. This was done by putting an inverted flower-pot over each plant, and there were many.

All four of us – our sister Anne and elder brother Michael as well as Brian and myself – took part in all this and we were allowed so many minutes' 'free-for-all' amongst the soft fruit, of which we took full advantage. We also had a pony, taking it in turns to ride, and Brian naturally enjoyed his share.

We had an old gardener named Robinson and if my mother spotted some signs of 'predators' in the kitchen garden he would say, 'Birds, madam – two-legged birds.'

After the war, my father came home and life returned to normal until 1922 when, on our summer holiday at Bude, Father was tragically drowned trying to rescue a family friend who had got into difficulties. Shortly after this, Little Offley was sold and we moved, eventually, to another lovely house, on lease, in Herefordshire – Hellens at Much Marcle.

By then, Brian had joined me at our preparatory school, Temple Grove in Eastbourne. A good school but austere and with terrible food. Here, I think, Brian started his love for cricket, inspired, no doubt, by the performances of Douglas Bader (better known as Group Captain Douglas Bader, DSO, DFC) who used to score century after century against other schools, earning us many an evening off work.

In the holidays, Brian was now old enough to walk with us to church, two miles every Sunday, no wheels allowed. For this, we boys were dressed in sailor suits. The Navy then was very much admired and respected by all. No doubt it was thought that this might encourage one of us to join that service.

We were at Much Marcle for about five years during which time Brian joined me at Eton where he made many friends, some of whom went up to Oxford with him.

From now on his main interest was cricket. He was a good player and became a good wicket-keeper. His ambition was to play for Eton at Lord's. Unfortunately the existing wicket-keeper stayed on an extra year and deprived him of his chance. A great disappointment.

During the holidays at Much Marcle, it was hunting in the winter and cricket, nothing but cricket, in the summer. He played for the village and at several country houses nearby. We also went to every point-to-point within reach and Brian greatly enjoyed the tipsters and the entertainers.

We had an amusing game we used to play at Hellens. The Ledbury to Ross-on-Wye road passed the Lodge gates and on Bank Holidays we took our old, bull-nosed Morris car to the road, drove it across the verge and made my sister lie down on the grass with tomato sauce liberally applied to her face and arms. The traffic was quite heavy for those days and a large number of kindly people stopped to ask if they could help. The 'accident' always worked.

Oxford was nothing but fun for him and he made many more friends, played more cricket – and more practical jokes.

One friend – I think it was William Douglas-Home – had a car and when he committed some minor traffic offence his university licence was temporarily removed. So he and Brian hired a horse-drawn carriage and went up and down the busy High Street, inevitably causing the most appalling traffic jams. Going very slowly with a horse was no offence. Thus they took their revenge.

When Brian had a lunch party in his rooms, he had an arrangement with his scout, a splendid man called Sid Honey. When lunch was in progress, Sid would come in and say, 'Sir, a lady stands without.'

To which Brian would reply, 'Without what?'

'Sir, without food or clothing.'

'Give her food and bring her in.'

A similar line was taken once when he was lunching with our sister at her home in Hertfordshire.

Before lunch, the cook, a delightful character called Emily Dawson, came into the room and said to my sister, 'Would you like the tart hot or cold?'

Brian chipped in, 'Bring her in just as she is!'

When he was at New College it was sometimes necessary to climb back in – quite a tricky process over the normal route. So Brian and William kept their eyes open and discovered that the coal man delivered through a side gate in the big wall, for which he had a key. They noted that when delivering he left the key in the lock so they prepared a mould in a flat tin and when his back was turned removed the key and took an imprint. The problem was solved!

Shortly after this I went abroad to join my regiment and saw very little of Brian for some years, but his life went on in the same happy way – always kind and entertaining, making friends and other people happy.

There is one example of his rapid wit which I think is typical of him: after Oxford he went into the London office of the family coffee business and after a time was sent to the Brazilian office. One morning, after a late night, he was late at the office and his immediate boss was not pleased.

Boss: 'You are late. It is now 9.30 and you should have been here at 8.30.'

Brian: 'Why? What happened?'

Caroline Douglas-Home

The Honourable Caroline Douglas-Home knew Brian as a long-time friend of her uncle, William, and of both her parents, Lord Home, the former Prime Minister, and Elizabeth, Lady Home, who had known Brian as a schoolboy at Eton. Lady Home's father, Dr Cyril Alington, was head-master of the school in Brian's day.

Brian Johnston was twelve days younger than, and a very great friend of, my father's brother, William, the playwright, who died in September, 1992. He had also known my mother well while he was at Eton and afterwards, and was godfather to my younger sister, Meriel.

During Meriel's wedding reception, an extremely large guest put herself and three others into our lift, designed to carry four average-sized people.

The lift's safety system came into action and it stopped between floors.

It had only recently been installed and although it had a release brake we were worried that it might plummet two floors with disastrous results so my brother and I set about winding it down manually.

Brian heard what was happening, stationed himself with a glass of champagne outside the doors to which the lift was being lowered and proceeded to give a running commentary on its progress.

It was as if a full-scale emergency potholing rescue was taking place!

He started by wondering about the state of health of 'these brave people who have been in this predicament for about fifteen minutes,' and progressed to, 'Can I? Yes, I think I can; yes, I can, I can see the floor of the car and feet and it looks as though they are all managing to remain upright. No-one has fainted.

'Given another few inches, we will be able to revive these incredibly brave and calm people with glasses of champagne.

'Another inch or two and the doors will be able to be opened and they will no doubt fall into the arms of their friends and relations who have been waiting anxiously outside the gates for thirty minutes.

'Hurrah, the gates have been opened to emotional scenes of relief and gratitude to their rescuers.'

It was hilarious at the time and the one thing *everyone* remembered about the reception!

Brian was involved in another incident which did not cause quite so much hilarity when my mother and Aunt Rachel, my father's sister, drove home to Eton after visiting all their friends in Oxford and spent the journey discussing them all in often not very complimentary or discreet terms.

After driving into the garage where they continued their conversation they were horrified when Brian and a friend suddenly burst out from where they had somehow managed to conceal themselves in the back of the car.

My mother and aunt were really furious with them and it was nearly the end of their friendship!

Over the years – on birthdays or just because he thought of him regularly since he became ill – Brian has sent my father 'Blackpool Pier' postcards, the dirtier the better. And the *Evening with Johnners* tapes have given him great pleasure since he was given them as a Christmas present.

Brian's address at Uncle William's memorial service began, 'I had always hoped that William would do for me what I am sad but honoured to be doing now for him. I especially wanted him because I knew that he would be kind, generous and witty.'

2
THE COFFEE BREAK

It is hard to believe now but Brian might never have been a broadcaster and entertainer at all if his family had had their way. They wanted him to go into the old Johnston coffee business.

Only Brian could tell the tale and this is his account from his book, Someone Who Was *(Methuen London, 1992), reprinted by permission of Reed Consumer Books.*

The song was quite right. There *is* an awful lot of coffee in Brazil. There was in 1842 too, when my great-grandfather Edward Johnston founded the firm of E. Johnston to export coffee from Santos in Brazil.

The firm went through the usual periods of success and depression common to all businesses. It was later formed into a group of companies under the name Brazilian Warrant, and in the late twenties and thirties suffered badly from the collapse of the Brazilian currency and such overproduction of coffee that much of it had to be burnt.

The family business, in which we still had shares, was always in the background of my early life. There had, however, not been a member of the Johnston family in it since my father died in 1922. They always tried to tempt myself or one of my two brothers back into the fold.

This was the position in 1934 when I was due to come down from Oxford with no other job prospect in mind. I secretly had no wish to join it, but as there was no immediate alternative – I had toyed with the idea of being a schoolmaster or even an actor – I weakened and started my business career with the Brazilian Warrant in October 1934.

So I became a white-collar boy, and each day like countless others I put my bowler hat on my head, my umbrella on my arm, and caught a tube train at the same time each morning from South Kensington station. Each day as I got into the train there was always one thought on my mind – was I in the same carriage as the 'Nodder'? I had given this name to a man who always travelled to the City at the same time. Whether the poor chap had a disease or not I don't know but I used to watch him, fascinated. He just sat reading the paper, sometimes nodding his head vigorously up and down as if in agreement with what he was reading, at other times shaking it from one side to the other as if he couldn't disagree more. It was very funny to watch and brightened those otherwise dull and crowded journeys.

For the first year in the City I started at what is known as 'the bottom'. That applied to my salary too! I learnt to type with one finger (or two if in a hurry), I made up contracts, decoded cables, and was introduced to such financial intricacies as 'draft at ninety days' sight' or 'cash against documents less 2½ per cent'. I know that some people understand these sorts of things, but I never did. I was also taught how to taste coffee. A fascinating business – one dips a spoon into a cup of piping hot coffee (no sugar or milk!), swills it around in the mouth and spits it out into a huge spittoon. I must admit I have often wanted to do this to some of the coffee one gets in England – even with sugar and milk! I soon learnt to nod my head wisely and pretend I knew which was good and which was bad. This constant sipping, alas, played havoc with the digestion. Although I enjoyed myself during this time I'm afraid I cannot pretend I enjoyed my job.

One of the other chaps who shared an office with me used to toss me for sixpence a time. We'd put down all the coins we had in our pockets and call heads or tails on the lot. One day we had all the coins down on the desk when we heard footsteps from the Chairman's office two doors away. I quickly covered the coins with an important letter and pretended to be discussing it with my colleague. Of course it was just this letter that the Chairman had come along to read. He came in and picked it up and there were all our coins lying guiltily in front of him. What he thought I do not know, but were our faces red!

After a year in the City I went to an agent in Hamburg for three months to learn a little German and something about the coffee trade there. This was in 1935 and even then our agent and his staff had to be members of the Nazi Party or (so they said) they wouldn't be given an import licence for coffee. I learnt a little German, and also to shake hands all round in the office on arrival in the morning, on going to and coming back from lunch, and again when we went home in the evening. One evening I was taken by these Nazis to a Party rally in a huge indoor sports hall to hear Goebbels speak. I didn't understand what he was saying but my friends translated from time to time. It was his famous 'guns or butter' speech and it was really terrifying to be a very obvious Englishman in civilian clothes, standing there among those shouting and cheering Nazis in uniform. At that time the small country of Memel was annoying the Nazis. I remember Goebbels saying it was just like a fly on one's nose: 'We shall flick it off when we can't stand it any more!'

After Hamburg I was packed off in 1936 to Brazil to learn the business at that end. It was a lovely voyage of seventeen days or so, calling at Lisbon on the way. It was my first time out of Europe and I revelled in the sunshine which became hotter and hotter as we went south. My destination was Santos, where our head office was, and the day before arriving there we had the thrill of entering Rio harbour at night with the magnificent illuminated figure of Christ looking down from thousands of feet above the entrance of the harbour. Rio itself is a lovely city – bathed in sunshine, with luxurious shops and hotels, beautiful women, golden sands, lively nightclubs – all right, I'll stop, but it's true. You ask anyone who has been there.

Santos is very different. It's a busy port, exporting coffee and cotton in fantastic quantities, but with little to offer in the way of entertainment except a beach, and few people live there for fun. It's a place for work, and Americans, Europeans and Brazilians alike did work very hard. There was a small English colony there, and quite a few Americans, and I soon settled down among them to learn more about coffee and quite a lot about life.

While there I had my first experience of acting and producing. I had always loved the theatre, especially revue and variety, but had never performed in public, reserving my attempts at being funny for my friends. In Brazil there were no other distractions except work, so we produced several revues and cabarets, and I even acted the 'funny man' in *The Ghost Train*. This was produced by James Joint who was the British Consul in Santos at the time. He later became the Commercial Attaché at Buenos Aires, and the man who, by a strange coincidence, negotiated with the Argentinians over the meat question! When I knew him he unfortunately had no children, or else I'm sure they would have been known as the 'two veg'!

Besides playing quite a bit of cricket on matting, our American friends initiated us into the art of baseball and every Sunday morning the Limeys used to play the Yanks on the beach. Then came the great day when an American cruiser visited Santos and we challenged them to a proper game on the cricket ground. Imagine what a thrill I had when I went in and scored a home run. What a different game from cricket. When I went in the catcher kept up a running commentary: 'Come on boys, this Limey's no good, he'll never hit a thing, he's easy meat, heck I believe he's nervous . . .' and so on. Naturally enough I missed the first two balls the pitcher sent down, but the constant chatter spurred me to better things, and at the third (my last chance) I let fly and luckily connected. The ball went soaring to where in cricket mid-off and extra cover would be fielding. For some unknown reason the Americans had no-one out there, and by the time they retrieved the ball I had completed a home run, or rounder to anyone who doesn't know baseball. But oh, if only the wicket-keeper was allowed to talk like that in cricket. It would be too easy – I believe I would have played for England!

There was a large German colony there, who were most aggressive at the time. One man we particularly disliked used to travel to work on the same tram and we suspected him of being a spy. Herr Kurl was his name, and imagine our delight one day when he took his hat off and we saw that he was as bald as a coot!

I made several journeys inland to visit fazendas and coffee and cotton plantations. Except for the big towns, São Paulo, Rio, Santos, Bahía, etc., the country is very primitive and some of the main roads are little better than sand tracks. In the really hot weather (December to April) journeying by car was a nightmare because of the terrible dust. I didn't know this when I was given a job soon after I arrived, to meet a very important American buyer at the docks. His liner was only calling in on its way to Buenos Aires and we'd been warned that he and his family would like a trip inland. So I ordered a car for them, and as it was a lovely fine day made sure it was an open tourer. They set off happily enough, smartly dressed, the American buyer in white panama and Palm-Beach suit, and his wife in the latest model from New York. I was waiting for them when they came back in the evening and I got the shock of my life. It might have been the Ink Spots going to a funeral. Their faces were black with dust and their clothes just one dark mess. I'm afraid we never got another order from that American buyer.

I had my first experiences, too, of the Carnival – when everyone goes mad for three days on end. All business is stopped and the streets are crowded with singing, dancing people. It is a fantastic and quite unbelievable sight to English eyes. They just never stop, in spite of the terrific heat, often nearly 100°F in the shade – if you can find the shade. The revelry goes on all night too, with bands playing non-stop, no intervals and everyone just dancing round the room in long or short lines, like the Palais Glide. All the dancers, too, carry scent sprays which they squirt continuously over each other.

It was after one of these Carnivals when I had been in Santos for about eighteen months that I was struck down by a disease, quite common out there, called acute peripheral neuritis. I found my legs and arms gradually becoming paralysed, and in about two days was completely immobile.

I had to recuperate for six months before rejoining the firm in London round about the time of the Munich Crisis – I was given the title of London Manager, but still knew little about coffee, nor, to be honest, cared about it. I was sent on a short tour of our European agents which enabled me to visit Norway, Sweden and Denmark as well as France, Belgium and Holland. But the trip also included Hamburg just before Christmas. My friends in the office there still made me welcome but there was a nasty feeling of militancy and aggression in the attitude of everyone I met. I was glad to get back to my usual Christmas stocking. I soldiered on until the following September when war was declared. I felt a sense of relief and as I left to join up I made it quite plain to everyone in the office that I would never return to the coffee business.

3
THE WAR YEARS

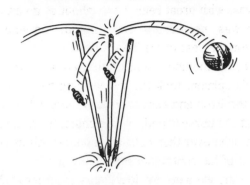

In his many books, Brian Johnston has given detailed accounts of his time
in the Grenadier Guards, of how he progressed from the reserve to the Royal
Military College at Sandhurst, of how he spent four years during the war as a
Technical Adjutant in the Guards Armoured Division before being promoted
to Major with special responsibility for welfare.

Yet nowhere does he describe how he won the Military Cross for bravery
in some of the great battles, preferring to say with typical modesty, 'I was
only the Technical Adjutant and although from my own point of view I was
often too damn close I was not one of those actually fighting the battles in
the tanks. They are the people best qualified to tell the tale . . .'

Two of the men who served with him were Lords Carrington and Whitelaw
and they have their own special memories.

Lord Carrington

Peter Carrington, the Foreign Secretary in Mrs Thatcher's first adminis-
tration, and later Secretary-General of NATO, played cricket with Brian

*Johnston and served with him in the Grenadier Guards. Brian could never
take playing cricket, or preparing for war, completely seriously . . .*

Before the war, my father used to run a private cricket team at our house
in Devonshire. This was the first time I met Brian, who had recently left
Oxford and was, with great reluctance, about to go into the family coffee
business. He was, needless to say, the life and soul of the party and
remained so for the rest of his life.

There were, I remember, some rather earnest cricketers in the team
who, in Brian's opinion, took the whole thing far too seriously. I agreed
with him. At the Eton and Harrow match, he used to sit on top of a particular stand at the nursery end, barracking both wittily and provocatively
all Harrovians, whatever they did, to the general disapproval of the elderly
and the delight of his contemporaries.

During the war, we were for four years together in the same battalion
of the Grenadiers. When the battalion was converted from infantry to
armoury, he was for some obscure reason chosen to be the Technical
Adjutant. Even after numerous courses, I am not sure just how much I
understood of the workings of the internal combustion engine! But just
the sight of Brian when your tank had broken down arriving in a scout
car named F.U.J.I.A.R. – an acronym that can be deciphered by all his
fellow Grenadiers – was in itself enough to lift the spirits.

Everybody had a nickname. His Technical Sergeant who had a rather
sallow complexion was named Gandhi, and though without any of his name-
sake's characteristics, was most gratified; not so perhaps, the intelligence
officer who delighted in giving us rather portentous briefings on the wider
aspects of the campaign and was immediately and for ever after known as
the 'bigger picture'; and Neville Berry, 'the Hatchet' (oh dear). And, of
course, Brian organized all the entertainment and took part in it himself.

On one occasion after the war, Brian and I met at a dinner in Govern-
ment House, Adelaide, on the occasion of a Test match between England
and Australia. That afternoon, Colin Cowdrey, I think, had been given out
by what Brian had thought to be a most deplorable decision. Whilst playing
billiard fives after a very convivial dinner, Brian shouted across to Don
Bradman that 'the umpire had clearly never played cricket in his life,' and

that the decision that afternoon was farcical. Sir Donald lost his temper and, spluttering with rage, replied, 'How dare you speak like that! Why _____ used to open the innings for South Australia until his eyesight failed!'

How Brian did enjoy that, and how we enjoyed Brian. We shall miss him.

Lord (Willie) Whitelaw

The Rt. Hon. The Viscount Whitelaw, KT, CH, MC, the distinguished and long-serving Cabinet Minister, formerly deputy leader of the Conservative Party and now its eminence grise, *experienced with Brian the early days of the Guards Armoured Division.*

I retain a clear memory of a tank incident at Bovington, when Brian and I, for some reason totally unknown, were put on a Technical Adjutants Course when the Guards Armoured Division was formed.

At one point in our course we all had to take an engine to pieces and put it together again. When we had finished, Brian turned to me and asked, 'How many bolts have you got left?'

'A pocketful,' I said.

'So have I,' he said.

These, of course, were bolts which should be put into the engine before it was fully restored and we had failed to find a place to put them. Brian then turned to me and said, 'Give me your bolts and we will put them into Uppers' pockets.' ('Uppers' was in fact Sir Gerald Upjohn, at that time a very distinguished barrister and latterly a judge.) The bolts were put in his pockets and we all stood to our engines. Amazingly enough, Brian's started despite the lack of bolts, and so, even more amazingly, did mine. When we were asked the question, 'How many bolts have you got in your pockets?' we answered, 'None, Sir,' in both cases.

Then the Officer in Charge turned to Gerald Upjohn and said, 'How many bolts have you got?'

'None, Sir,' he replied.

'Turn out your pockets, sir.'

He turned out his pockets and there were all the bolts. The horrified Officer in Charge finished, 'Sir, from you, a leading figure at the Bar!'

Brian and I then took fright and said, 'Oh, but Sir, it was our fault, we put the bolts that we had left into Major Upjohn's pockets.'

At that moment, another friend spoke up. It was William Douglas-Home, well known to everyone, with a strong sense of humour. 'Put these wicked officers in the jail. Put them in the jail. They are very bad men.'

To which the Officer, by this time fed up, said, 'If you go on, we will put you all in jail.' But still, he never believed it.

When we received our reports sent back to our Regiments, they all had the same phrase, 'These officers appear to be unsound under pressure.' Perhaps, not something, I think, which would have been subscribed either to Brian or to me over the years which have passed since then.

Martin Rowson

4

HELLO AUNTIE

Robert Hudson

Robert Hudson, once described by Brian Johnston as 'the broadcaster's commentator' because he made the job sound so easy, knew Brian as a friend, a colleague and a boss – as Head of Radio Outside Broadcasts.

Brian joined the BBC Outside Broadcasts Department on 13 January 1946, having survived the war with distinction and also, after demobilization, two microphone tests set by the revered Head of Radio 'OBs', Seymour de Lotbinière ('Lobby' for short: in fact he was 6'8"!).

First, Brian had to record his impression of Piccadilly Circus, as if speaking to servicemen and women still serving overseas; incidentally, I was one of his mythical audience, still stuck in the Far East. Secondly, he was to cajole some sensible replies from reluctant interviewees in Oxford Circus.

Later, in the same year, having acquired my own 'demob' suit, I made my first contact with the BBC – a twenty-minute recorded 'audition' as a cricket commentator at Lord's. John Arlott was giving one of his first 'live' broadcasts on the same match, and I remember thinking that I might stand a chance if the BBC could accept such a pronounced Hampshire burr!

Brian and I shared a television broadcast for the first time on 14 and 15 August 1948, at the Oval, when Don Bradman, needing just four runs for a Test match average of 100, was bowled by Eric Hollies for a duck. This was followed by a number of televised county matches in the late forties and early fifties, which we shared as commentators on a virtually 'ball-by-ball' basis. There wasn't much else on, in the afternoons, in those days! Our commentary position at the Oval was on the flat roof of a stand next to the pavilion. It consisted of a table, three chairs and a monitor screen. Access was by ladder. Our scorer was Roy Webber, who didn't relish the climb up, weighed down by reference books.

The opening of the Sutton Coldfield transmitter allowed television to leave London for the first time. In July 1950, Brian and I went up to Trent Bridge, Nottingham, for the England v. West Indies Test match. In those days, the occupants of houses bordering the ground could get a good view of the match from their balconies. Surprisingly, on this occasion, all the balconies were empty. Brian suggested, on the air, that anyone watching the match on TV should come out and give us a wave. In next to no time the balconies were full of waving 'viewers'. We went round to meet some of them at close of play; television had certainly 'arrived' in the Midlands!

During this period, Brian had begun his series of *Let's Go Somewhere* broadcasts as part of the popular *In Town Tonight* radio programme. In these, he found himself, each week, in some improbable, and sometimes dangerous, situations. The broadcasts were always 'live', so anything could happen, and very often did. Only someone with Brian's insatiable love of practical jokes, combined with a high degree of professionalism at the microphone, could have carried it off.

Sometimes, we would be together at a televised cricket match in the afternoon, and Brian would ask me to take the last period of commentary, so that he could slip away to the chosen venue of that week's escapade, which, of course, was not revealed in the *Radio Times*. He never told me where he was going, and it was quite a shock to switch on that evening and to hear my co-commentator of a few hours before in the role of a trainee waiter at a well-known West End restaurant, spilling the soup over guests (invited by the BBC) to test their 'politeness threshold'.

The series was very popular, and Brian became well known long before his *Test Match Special* days, for which he is generally remembered today. Among many other things, he was shaved on stage by the Crazy Gang, put into a state of hysterical laughter by a hypnotist, rode a horse in a circus, and sold matches in the Strand, while singing 'It's a long way to Tipperary'. He collected sixpence-halfpenny (in the old money), to which the OB engineer added one penny as a signal that he had fifteen seconds left. On another occasion he was immured, a little shakily, in the Chamber of Horrors at Madame Tussaud's.

When Brian placed an advertisement in the evening papers, chaos reigned in Lower Regent Street when the roadway was jammed by young ladies replying. In the advertisement he had invited them to meet 'well set-up young gentleman, with honourable intentions, identified by red carnation and blue and white spotted scarf'. The code word was 'How's your uncle?' As Brian appeared, attired as advertised, on the steps of the Criterion Restaurant, with traffic at a standstill and the police not best pleased, there was a massive shout of 'How's your uncle?'

Brian had had leanings towards a stage career. For his hundredth appearance on *In Town Tonight* he was allowed by Peter Duncan, the producer, to perform a cross-talk act with John Ellison as the 'straight man'. This turned out to be full of the excruciating jokes in which, together with slightly risqué postcards, Brian took a particular delight.

If you can bear it, here is part of the script.

B.J. We don't want London Bridge any longer.
J.E. Why not?
B.J. It's long enough already.

B.J. It is all in the papers tonight.
J.E. What is?
B.J. Fish and chips.

B.J. I've got a goat with no nose.
J.E. Really? How does it smell?
B.J. Terrible.

In 1955, the idea of *Test Match Special* was born. I was broadcasting the Yorkshire v. Notts match at Scarborough in the North of England Home Service. Freddie Trueman did the hat-trick, with five seconds of our fixed twenty-five-minute broadcasting period to spare. Similar constriction applied, at that time, to Test match broadcasts, so I suggested to my boss in London that what was needed to avoid potential disaster was continuous ball-by-ball coverage of Test matches. The best place for this seemed to be on Network 3, as it was then called, which broadcast many hours of music, but had few listeners. After a predictable altercation with the music lovers, *Test Match Special* took to the air at Edgbaston on 30 May 1957, with the slogan 'Don't miss a ball, we broadcast them all', and we have done ever since.

At that time, Brian was a fixture in the TV commentary box and so took no part in the early days of *Test Match Special*. My own first appearance was at Old Trafford in 1958 with John Arlott and Freddie Brown as my fellow commentators, with expert comment from E.W. Swanton and Bill Merritt, the New Zealand Test cricketer.

In 1961, on the retirement from the staff of Rex Alston, I joined Brian Johnston and Raymond Baxter in London as a Staff Commentator – a dream occupation, if ever there was one. Relieved of all administrative and production duties, it was our job (and pleasure) to broadcast anything anywhere at any time, on either radio or TV. There were no set hours and certainly no overtime. We did whatever was required, within the security (if not the riches) of a staff salary.

The flexibility allowed us on occasion to exchange roles between radio and TV. The atmosphere in the TV commentary box was relaxed to say the least, especially when Brian and I were joined by Denis Compton. On one occasion, lack of communication with our producer in the van below, as the tea interval approached, led to a coded request for sustenance: 'Mention Freddie Trueman if you want a cup of tea,' said the voice in our headphones. 'I think it's time Trueman came on,' said Brian promptly. 'He will need at least two slips.' Result, a cup of tea with two lumps of sugar!

In the sixties, Brian was almost always on television with the excellent and reliable Peter West. Occasionally, however, he was part of the radio team, and I formed the impression then that radio was where he really belonged. I was proved right in 1970, when television decided that cricket had to be taken seriously. Ex-Test players would do the commentary, and levity was out.

The era of Richie Benaud was born.

One result of all this was that Brian was no longer required by TV. By that time, I was Head of Radio Outside Broadcasts, and thus Brian's boss. He came to see me in my office looking, for once, a trifle shaken. I was able to cheer him up by inviting him to join the *Test Match Special* team, not just for one match, but for all of them. The decision had taken me about five seconds!

As it happened, the visit of the South African team that year was cancelled, but we broadcast the substitute series against The Rest of the World, in full, on the radio. Brian broadcast all five matches. A new era had begun for *Test Match Special*: 'Johnners' had arrived.

Up to 1970, without being unduly serious, *Test Match Special* had stuck closely to the cricket and returned listeners to the studio for music when it rained. Now the programme found itself with two 'personalities' of contrasting styles in Brian and John Arlott; riches indeed, but someone else was needed with his feet firmly on the ground. This eventually proved to be Christopher Martin-Jenkins, and the team as a whole blossomed under the benevolent guidance of Peter Baxter, whom I had put in charge of cricket broadcasting in 1973.

Johnners was to stay with *Test Match Special* for the next twenty-three seasons, all but two of them after his official retirement from the BBC staff at the statutory age of sixty. Apart from anything else, it was a feat in the Peter Pan class to keep so mentally alert as the years went by. Ball-by-ball commentary is a tiring business, demanding total concentration when on the air, and a careful eye on the cricket when you are not. Yet at eighty-one Johnners sounded twenty years younger. Of course, he loved the job. Who wouldn't? He brought to it a love of cricket, and a zest for life, which not only rode the airwaves but lightened the atmosphere in the commentary box as well.

He had no exceptional command of words to compare with John Arlott, but his training had been well grounded under the tutelage of Lobby. He never missed a ball, and you always knew exactly what had happened to it. He burbled – I think that is the right word – with good

Bill Tidy

humour and benevolence. For Johnners, the sun shone out of everyone. I doubt if he had an enemy in the world. For me, as his boss, it was a tonic to have him in the department until he left the staff in 1972 – the best morale-raiser of all time.

Test Match Special attracted new listeners, who previously cared little for cricket. The large daily postbag often included cakes for Brian; somebody also wisely sent an antidote for tooth decay! The tone of the programme moved slightly down-market, from the respected to the popular. Our team of raconteurs and experts, among them Trevor Bailey and Fred Trueman, was encouraged to keep talking when Rain Stopped Play, and Audience Research, on at least one occasion, recorded an increase in listeners. The match itself was becoming superfluous!

Brian's activities were by no means confined to cricket. I was with him on many State and Royal occasions, including the marriage of Prince Charles in St Paul's Cathedral – but did he really say that the bride was going up the steps into the pavilion? A good story.

When the Queen, on her Silver Jubilee, walked from St Paul's to the Guildhall for lunch, Brian, following behind, microphone in hand, asked Prince Philip to say a few words. 'I'd like to,' he said, 'but I can't hear myself think!'

When Brian left the staff, I suggested that, following the death of Franklin Engelmann, he should take over the presentation of *Down Your Way*, which had for many years been produced by the OB Department. It was a gentle, uncontroversial programme which suited Brian well. It was not out to trick anyone nor ask them awkward questions. Brian had the gift of drawing people out in a cheerful reassuring way, which mirrored his own character.

I knew Brian for nearly half a century as a friend, as a colleague at the microphone, and finally as his boss. It was a privilege to have filled those three roles. He was a unique and lovely man. We shall not see his like again.

Lord Orr-Ewing

Ian Orr-Ewing, promoted to the House of Lords in 1971 after twenty years as MP for North Hendon, was a pioneer of televised cricket and the man responsible for introducing Brian to cricket commentary. He is President of Harrow Wanderers, oldest rivals of Brian's favourite club, the Eton Ramblers.

It was in July 1926 that I first met Brian Johnston. Appropriately enough, we were sitting alongside each other at Lord's where Eton were playing Harrow, as they have done since 1805. With a like-minded group of friends we sat above the sight screen at the nursery end. In those days, these were free seats known as Block G. Brian became the centre of appropriate and ribald comments.

Before the Second World War, the match was one of the highlights of the London season and all the ladies were dressed in their finery and men and boys alike in morning coats and top hats. After the war, these clothes were dropped. When the match was restarted in 1946, many of us attended wearing our demob suits, when there appeared behind us Aidan Crawley, who flying Hurricanes in the war was shot down and became a PoW. Later he was elected a Labour MP. He was a far better cricketer than any of us, having been twelfth man for England, and he was immaculately dressed. Brian spotted Crawley and quickly shouted, 'Jump back into the window of Moss Bros from whence you have evidently come!' Like all Brian's humour, it produced spontaneous laughter without a trace of viciousness. The many victims invariably led the laughter themselves.

In those early post-war summers, we held a number of matches at Hurlingham where Brian captained the Etonians and I captained the Block G Harrovians.

I was demobilized from the Royal Air Force in early 1946 and picked up my pre-war job in charge of outside broadcasts at the BBC TV headquarters at Ally Pally. Sport figured largely in our broadcasts and this included the Test matches at Lord's and the Oval, Wimbledon, Twickenham, Ascot and Wembley, and athletics from the White City. I was testing out new commentators and recontacting those with pre-war experience. I telephoned Brian, who had just joined the BBC in Portland Place, and asked him to do a cricket Test for me. He fitted like a glove.

Viewers were always entertained, even when the cricket was boring or rain stopped play. From day one, throughout all his broadcasts he gave a relaxed impression and was extremely professional, taking great pains and always being scrupulously punctual; the result of taking trouble and providing dedication to the task in hand.

Brian was one of the most generous and kind of men. It is a reflection of the thousands for whom he has provided help, laughter and fun that his memorial service was held at Westminster Abbey, giving us all the opportunity to thank him for the fine example he set.

Frank Coven

Frank Coven, former director of Associated Newspapers, enjoyed Brian's company for nearly fifty years – though their friendship was tested when Coven was working for a certain Kerry Packer as London and European Director of Channel Nine TV Network (Australia).

I was demobbed from the Army in 1945 – as was Brian – and I returned to the *Daily Mail* at about the same time he joined the BBC Outside Broadcasting Radio Unit.

I cannot place the exact moment I met Brian but I remember him well as one of an outstanding coterie of people which included the war correspondent Wynford Vaughan-Thomas, John Ellison, Henry Riddell and Peter Dimmock – the latter however being more involved in television commentating and production activities. The famous Richard Dimbleby, returned to the BBC from his reporting exploits during the war, was also beginning to make his mark at this time. I have never known such an atmosphere of bonhomie and enthusiasm as existed amongst these colleagues, and already Brian was commencing to shine within this group.

At that period I was in charge of entertainment and broadcasting for the *Daily Mail* Ideal Home Exhibition, and soon, of public relations for the Associated Newspapers Group. In these capacities I inevitably came in contact with the BBC personalities I have mentioned and Brian, Richard Dimbleby, Wynford Vaughan-Thomas and Peter Dimmock in particular.

I remember Brian's first engagements in the BBC Saturday night radio feature *In Town Tonight* directed by the much respected Peter Duncan, and the latter's delight in the stunts that Brian performed – some of them dangerous as well as comic.

In 1947 I recollect meeting, for the first time, his eventual wife Pauline with Brian and her father as they entered the Dorchester Hotel as I was leaving it. To those who have met her themselves I need not say how beautiful she was and how attractive she remains to this day. All who know her will be aware of her steadfastness and support of Brian throughout his married life.

I look back upon uproarious parties at Brian's house – his fun and laughter outstanding as usual – and one particularly intimate and delightful dinner with Brian, Pauline, my wife Edwina and the late Sir Martin Gilliat, the Private Secretary to the Queen Mother, who was at Eton with Brian. Edwina's and my own dinners at the Ideal Home Exhibition for Brian and Pauline and our by now firm BBC friends will also remain in my memory.

I remember too the marvellous garden cricket parties at the Johnstons at Test match times at which it was very interesting to meet so many famous cricketers. In this connection I recollect Kerry Packer, for whom I was London director, saying to me, when discussing the revolution he caused in the world of cricket, 'As a pom, Frank, you won't like this much, and I wouldn't have more to do with it than you have to.' When I told Brian of the conversation he said, 'I should think not!' Although I believe his attitude softened as he appreciated eventually that after all certain benefits did emerge from this upheaval.

Concerning prominent personalities my mind turns to a remarkable incident involving Gilbert Harding and Brian. Gilbert, who was an outstanding interviewer, commentator and performer and a possessor of great charm, could also be somewhat eccentric. At one of our *Daily Mail* Television Banquets for no reason whatsoever he turned upon Brian and was violently rude to him. However, instead of reciprocating Brian accepted this with the utmost calmness and the matter was closed. Except, as Brian later told me, the next morning, as was quite typical of Gilbert, he phoned to offer his deep apologies which were, of course, immediately accepted.

The *Daily Mail* ran a series of Channel Swim races and these naturally appealed particularly to Brian. On one occasion the two of us swam quite a distance in the race with Pauline supervising from a rowing boat. This Brian said reminded him of bathing days at his prep school Temple Grove which was in Eastbourne, and fairly recently we visited the site of the school which is now, I believe, a dental college. As happens to all of us on these occasions I think that Brian was somewhat moved.

My last project in the essential company of Brian was when Edwina was Chairman of the Corporation of London's celebrations of the 800th Anniversary of the Mayoralty, and one of the outstanding features of this was a repetition of Dick Whittington's walk from Pauntley in Gloucestershire to the City of London. We arranged with Brian and Pauline to meet us in Windsor whence we set out to meet Dick and his cat on their journey. This we did and amongst admiring vocal crowds Brian walked some distance with the two of them.

Better was to follow, however. We repaired to an adjacent field where with the eager assistance of various small boys Brian kept wicket, Dick Whittington bowled and the cat batted! Absolutely glorious. I can think of no better memory of Brian at his very best than on that particular morning. What a lovely man he was.

5

ON THE BOX

Peter West

Peter West and Brian Johnston were the familiar, friendly and proficient core of the television cricket commentary team for most of the fifties and sixties. Peter might have been the 'straight' man but he was not above a practical joke or two himself.

I had the good luck to work with Brian on televised cricket for the best part of twenty years. It would be hard indeed to think of a colleague more cheerful or cheering, more flexible or unselfish. It was quite simply a joy to be in the same commentary box, ineffable puns and all.

There have been so many shining and thoughtful tributes saluting his memory that it is not at all easy to emphasize one or two of his qualities which may have been lightly sketched.

Would they include, I wonder, his modesty and his utterly genuine humility? He was always totally, irrepressibly and unrepentantly himself: what you saw or heard was exactly what you got. Many attributes brought him the respect or admiration of the nation but surely it was his humility which won him its affection.

This brief personal reminiscence about a lovely and lovable man must include the story of a practical joke that Brian hatched one day during the Canterbury cricket week. His accomplice – no-one more willing – was the Kent and England batsman, Peter Richardson. As arranged, when I surreptitiously waved a handkerchief from the commentary box – signifying that Jim Swanton had taken up the microphone – Peter told the umpire that the booming noise was disturbing his concentration. So the umpire, whose name alas now escapes me, solemnly walked to the boundary underneath our box and conveyed the batsman's complaint. Brian got a fit of the giggles, rejoicing that he had managed to bring a first-class game of cricket to a temporary halt.

We enjoyed pulling Jim Swanton's leg but let me add that he took it – as always – in good part and that I have never tuned in to a better summarizer of a day's cricket.

It was not so long after this incident that Brian was dropped by BBC Television without so much as a warning or a thank-you letter for services rendered. The same thing happened to Denis Compton. It stuck in the craws of two men entitled to expect better – should one say old-fashioned? – treatment, and I'm not in the least surprised.

But in Brian's case it enabled Robert Hudson, Head of Radio Outside Broadcasts, to reclaim him as one of their own and to restore him to his true *métier*.

E.W. Swanton

E.W. 'Jim' Swanton, CBE, for many years doyen of English cricket writers was also a magisterial radio commentator and TV summarizer, who shared with Brian a deep affection for cricket – and many a broadcast.

My very first remembrance of Brian was of that prominent proboscis hovering over the stumps when I was batting on the New College ground at Oxford. That was in the early thirties when the University had a very high-class 'keeper in Peter Oldfield, good enough to be chosen in the Gentlemen and Players at Lord's. So Brian the undergraduate missed a blue just as, when a schoolboy, he had also failed to make the Eton XI. Nevertheless, he was a thoroughly capable wicket-keeper, always welcome in Eton Ramblers, Oxford Authentics, MCC and I Zingari sides.

I say MCC, for which he qualified as a player, but it was put about that his membership was officially delayed for a year because he was picked out as a ring-leader of a disorderly lot from both schools who used to trade badinage and genial insults with one another perched in the F and G blocks at the Nursery End during the Eton and Harrow match. When the last edition of the *Evening Standard* had gone to press, my report included, I used to go along and enjoy the exchanges. No-one had a sharper or readier wit than Brian: he was, in fact, a born comedian. As the butt of many of his stories – most with a basis of fact richly embellished – I used to taunt him with having incurred MCC's displeasure and he never positively denied it. Incidentally, it never worried me that he portrayed me as a pompous old Blimp: you couldn't take umbrage with Brian.

At the end of the war in Germany, Brian, who had won a Military Cross with the Grenadier Guards, with other like-minded spirits set about amusing the troops awaiting discharge or home posting with a series of revues, reputedly broad, outrageous and very funny. As compère, Brian was in his element, and it was then, if not earlier, that he decided to forsake the family coffee business in favour of his true *métier*.

In 1946 I carried on in sound broadcasting where I had left off in 1939, then with Howard Marshall and Michael Standing, now with Rex Alston and John Arlott. Brian, at first, was making his name in other outside programmes but when Ian (now Lord) Orr-Ewing recruited him to commentate on the fledgling TV service I was seconded to divide my Test appearances between sound and TV. In the early fifties the TV commentaries were in the hands of Peter West, Brian and me, with Bill Wright as the brilliant cameraman alongside us behind the bowler's arm. TV really took off surely in 1953 thanks to the Coronation and followed as it was with our coverage of the great Test match at the Oval. It was

Brian's good luck to be at the mike at the climax and to say, 'England have won – we've recovered the Ashes!'

Facilities in those early days were primitive to a degree. We sat at a card table on the edge of the flat pavilion roof from which a thermos once fell below, fortunately striking a Surrey member only a glancing blow. A little chap with a waxed moustache was perched nearby, meticulously scripting the score-card, a work of art that took time. Only when we got the thumbs-up from him could we say to the viewers: '. . . and now let's have a look at the score-card.'

As all now know, Brian was eventually relieved of his TV cricket commentating because he was thought to be too flippant. He took this hard at the time, naturally enough, because there was no word of thanks or appreciation of his pioneering work over many years. Retrospectively, of course, the decision was a blessing in disguise, for he was immediately snapped up by *Test Match Special* which his personality – coupled until 1980 with the contrasting genius of John Arlott – transformed into a national (indeed international) institution.

There has never been such a wide and prolonged expression of public grief at the death of a sporting figure as Brian provoked. In an age when decent people can only look askance at the personal lives of so many famous figures, here was an utterly good, benevolent, cheerful soul whose Christian qualities touched the hearts of millions. The cricket world especially has lost a dear friend. We shall remember him fondly, the one and only B.A.J.

Richie Benaud

The former Australian captain, who was to follow Brian into the television commentary box, describes how Johnners was thirty years ahead of his time.

Late in 1993 a cricket match with a difference was played at the 'Gabba in Brisbane. Billed as an Allan Border Tribute it drew an all-ticket capacity crowd of 18,000 spectators and was televised around Australia as part of a tribute year or, as it would be in England, a testimonial year for the Australian captain.

The difference was that, although played to a normal limited-overs formula, the telecast featured a number of experimental aspects such as mini-cameras in umpires' hats. That was only moderately successful, though interesting. There were also microphones on the players' collars and they wore tiny earpieces and were in communication with one another as well as with the television commentators.

It was, as you might gather, a slightly relaxed day rather than one where victory was paramount for either of the teams, Allan Border's XI and the Invitation XI. It also produced a lot of excellent cricket and was just about the best day of its type with which I have been connected. There was some lovely strokeplay and excellent bowling from former greats like Barry Richards, Joel Garner, Sir Richard Hadlee and others. The catch of the match, and very close to the catch of the season, was taken by ex-international Rugby League forward, Paul Vautin, who ran forty yards, hurled himself through the air and clung on to the ball. Later he said, 'Nothing remarkable about that, I just copied what I've been watching them do on television . . .'

More remarkable was the fact that everyone in Australia was so captivated by the thought of players being 'miked up' and able to talk with television commentators and to other players. You might think that in these days of extraordinary communications, television and computers, this should be commonplace but, in fact, it was first done by Brian Johnston around thirty years ago at Lord's in what, if memory serves me correctly, was a Lord's Taverners game. The two other participants were Denis Compton and your grey-haired correspondent, and each of us had in our trouser pockets a slightly cumbersome piece of equipment known as a 'backpak', and in one of our ears was an earpiece with a cable running to that equipment. There was also a microphone clipped to the front of each of our shirts.

It had been decided by Johnners and the producer that it would all work best when I was in the field and Denis was batting, and it was done without a rehearsal other than the 'Hello, can you hear me?' type. There were also a few soothing words such as, 'Don't worry, it'll be all right on the night.'

In fact, it turned out to be a revelation for television viewers and that was due to the panache, good humour and general organizing ability of Johnners and, behind the scenes, the producer. First of all Brian talked with Denis, and I was able, along with the television viewers, to hear the conversation. It was along the lines of what type of pitch was it, did Denis think I would be turning the ball a great deal, and how long was it since he had faced me at Lord's? Then I had a similar conversation with Brian.

When it came to my turn to bowl, Brian and the producer switched off the communication between Denis and me and we were talking only to Brian and the viewers about what we thought might happen and what we intended to do. It all worked perfectly, including the last over I bowled where I was nominating the type of stroke I would try to have him play, but he couldn't hear what I was murmuring to the viewers. The classic sweep shot was deliberately brought into play from the last two balls, one swept to the deep backward square leg boundary, the other, played even more cheekily, so fine that it raced away to the boundary in front of the Long Room!

It was a first, it was beautifully produced and the Johnston commentary was perfect.

When I was walking out of the Brisbane commentary box thirty years later, I was accosted by your everyday cricket follower who was enthused by what he had been watching, not only on the field but also on television in the 'Gabba Cricketers' Club a few yards away. 'That was the most marvellous thing I've seen. It must be great for you to be part of modern communications.'

When I told him we had done it at Lord's thirty years ago he looked at me as though I had taken leave of my senses. As I walked away I heard him say to his mate, 'Did you ever hear such rubbish? Isn't it sad about these former players when they reckon they've done it all before!'

Charles Griffin

6

TEST MATCH SPECIAL

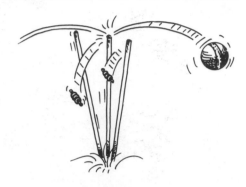

Peter Baxter

Brian Johnston was, of course, best known for Test Match Special. *Peter Baxter joined the team in 1966 and took over as producer in 1973.*

There was a persistent sound of trumpeting abroad in the corridors of Broadcasting House in the mid-sixties. No instrument was involved, beyond the lips of the tall genial figure who greeted everyone with a 'Good morning, old man.' (And I mean everyone. I can remember a female secretary or two being surprised by the address.) It would be delivered as boisterously to the most junior clerk as to the Director General himself. Thus could Brian Johnston in one walk down the passage both prick pomposity and boost morale. And that, when I joined the BBC was my first personal encounter with a man who I already, like so many others of his audience, felt I knew well from the radio.

At that time Brian was sharing a room in the Outside Broadcasts department which was dubbed the 'staff commentators' office' and included Raymond Baxter and Robert Hudson. What a rare mix of unquestioned, but very diverse, talent was there. When it came to cricket – and it was only a part of his busy schedule – he was still mostly on television for Test matches, but a frequent visitor to the likes of John Arlott, Alan Gibson, Norman Yardley and Freddie Brown in the radio box. Quite often for county cricket, particularly rounds of the Gillette Cup, he would be the studio link-man and even on a line from Broadcasting House his exuberance could lift the spirits of those reporting from round the country.

When he did settle in to *Test Match Special*, he became at once its moving force – the catalyst for almost everything that happened in the box. John Arlott may not have entirely approved the Johnners style, though I believe his concern was principally that others would try to ape it. There was, different as they were, a respect for the talent of the other from each and I cannot recall anything approaching a cross word between them. Perhaps Brian's gentle teasing was toned down a little for John, who would respond, when it came his way, with a forgiving twinkle of the eye. In fact, the arrival of Brian as a *Test Match Special* regular probably helped John to become known to a wider audience. It seemed in the seventies that the programme became the subject of many magazine features by writers who had just discovered it. While John – and a few others – have been masters of a choice phrase, perhaps reviewed in advance, Brian would sit down at the microphone and take events as he found them. Sometimes he would comment on a colleague's preparations for commentary, 'Oh, he makes me feel so guilty,' but he would himself always be armed, for instance, with a cutting of the national averages and have looked up some detail of a player that interested him.

He may have seemed to be the great amateur, but in so many things he was the most professional of them all, always the first to arrive and prepare for the day's play ahead and, for all the rather wearing and clichéd suggestions that he rambled on about chocolate cake incessantly, he really never did miss a ball. He was also always insistent on continuing to watch the game when he was not on the air.

Brian was, of course, not merely a cricket commentator. He had described other sports – show jumping and soccer among them – and many state occasions. I worked with him on a couple of royal weddings and the Queen's Silver Jubilee. So, when I was asked to take on the production of the Boat Race in 1980, the first post-John Snagge year for us, the first thing I did was to ring Brian and ask him to take over as the main commentator in the launch. He had, after all, operated by that time at every other conceivable point on the course. He was, incidentally, always keen to point out when we arrived at his favourite part of the river each year – Corney Reach. To that, as to any other broadcast he undertook, he brought life and boundless enthusiasm.

I took over the production of *Test Match Special* in 1973. I had known Brian for seven years by then, but it might have been a daunting task trying to run a programme which featured two household names like Johnston and Arlott. Neither ever made the job anything less than a pleasure and Brian was always a helpful guide if I had forgotten something in those early days, with a kindly intended dig like, 'Do you remember how good it was when we used to put the commentary rota up before play began?' So many of his jokes became familiar enough for us all to join in like a litany – none better than when anyone tried some foreign expression like *'joie de vivre'* or *'savoir faire'*. The inevitable reaction was always, 'How wise not to attempt the French accent,' commonly abbreviated by all of us to just 'How wise.'

There were gentle and subtle chidings for any colleague who in Brian's view went a bit too far. Christopher Martin-Jenkins described the apogee of a ball's flight and must have regretted it over the next ten minutes as the mutterings went on behind him. 'Apogee! What a good word. I wonder what he's talking about.' Henry Blofeld contributed a 'thoughtful' pigeon and never heard the last of it – 'Oh, there's one of Blowers' pigeons. Having a bit of a think, I expect.' It was Johnners who was probably most responsible for the reputation acquired by *Test Match Special* for talking on in the rain. (Rather less encouraged these days.) It came about during the Lord's Test of 1976. On the Saturday morning the match against the West Indies was critically poised. The gates were closed, the ground packed in anticipation of a great day's play in that memorably hot and dry summer, but as the umpires came out a faint sprinkling of rain began. It was never so heavy that play could not have started immediately it ceased. But it persisted – and so did the commentary team. Brian led it. John Arlott, normally the first to suggest a return to the studio in such a situation, became eager to join in and took on the baton with fascinating historical insights and a day on which no cricket was played at all at Lord's was enlivened by a rolling discussion, occasionally given fresh impetus by a listener's letter, but more often feeding on itself and periodic changes of participant. The public reaction was remarkable and added to by Brian arriving in the box on Monday morning, hugely amused by his own name-dropping as he said, 'My friends at the Palace tell me the Duke of Edinburgh thought we were rather good on Saturday.'

In 1980 we started on *Test Match Special* a lunchtime interview called 'A View from the Boundary'. The ground rules were that guests had to be well-known personalities with a love for the game of cricket, but no professional connection with it. The playwright Ben Travers was the guest who inspired it and others who have taken part have included the Duke of Edinburgh, the prime minister, John Major, Paul Getty and the former Archbishop of Canterbury, Lord Runcie. We have had actors, singers, hostages, politicians, footballers and comedians. At the outset the broad plan was to move the interviewing round the commentary team. John Arlott, for instance, joined in on the Ben Travers 'View' and Don Mosey talked to Patrick Moore. But it soon became clear that the session settled so naturally on Brian and the subjects were so eager to talk to him that he took it over altogether. He finished his last one in August 1993 at the Oval singing 'Underneath the Arches' with Roy Hudd, being for a minute or two the music hall artiste he would have loved to be.

It is, as I have said, an old cliché, but *Test Match Special*'s cake consumption must inevitably decline in future. Not that Brian was any more addicted to them than anyone else, but it was almost always to him that they were sent (as was more than half of our postbag) and it probably had something to do with his punctiliousness in thanking the senders on the air. I did sometimes have to check him by pointing out that if Alphonse's Cake Shoppe were sending us one of their wares, they were rather hoping for an on-the-air plug which would contravene our charter. 'Oh, but it's so nice of them,' he would exclaim. Indeed, that was his usual reaction as he opened his letters: 'Aren't people kind!' Every day he would sit in the commentary box opening a huge pile and getting them all read and sorted before play began. In the days of Test match rest days Sundays would often find him in a nearby public park scrawling answers to as many letters as he could.

I suppose for all of us the abiding memory will be of the ready wit and that extraordinarily infectious laugh which could reduce all who heard it to helpless mirth, as when someone sent us a copy of the Israeli Cricket Association's handbook. As he looked through the record section, Brian's eye lighted on the names of the pair who had put up the highest stand for the tenth wicket for Israel, Solly Katz and Benny Wadwaker. This tickled him so much that the tears of laughter rolled down his cheeks and as he wheezed away, trying to keep quiet in the commentary box, Don Mosey, attempting to describe the cricketing action in front of him, became all too aware of the paroxysms of mirth behind him and, without having the slightest idea what had caused this condition, found himself also rendered incapable of coherent speech as he succumbed to the infection of that laugh.

The Johnston wit was razor sharp. No opportunity for a pun was missed. Every day was fun to B.J. It will be the best tribute to his memory if the tremendous generosity of his spirit can be preserved in the *Test Match Special* commentaries.

Rex Alston

Rex Alston, ninety-two and still going strong despite having his obituary erroneously published in The Times *nearly ten years ago, is the longest-lived sports broadcaster of them all. Like all who worked alongside Brian, he remembers both his humour and his kindness.*

I joined the BBC in 1941 as an administrative officer but as I had had no experience of this type of work, having been a schoolmaster all my working life, it wasn't long before the BBC decided I would do better as a 'speaker' and I was transferred to Outside Broadcasting. About a year or so later someone by the name of Brian Johnston appeared in the department and was given a variety of jobs to do including organizing theatre broadcasts, at which he seemed to be very good. I was appointed to look after the BBC's cricket broadcasting and Brian soon made it known to me that his first love was cricket. Although he was a dear friend for over fifty years, we didn't perform together on many occasions, but I do recall one when he was in charge of a live outside broadcast about caving and I was the muggins who was sent down into the cave. While we were on the air he spoke to me and instead of my response heard the sound of running water. This brought forth the comment from Brian, 'That was my colleague who is extremely nervous!'

We didn't do many cricket broadcasts together but I remember one occasion when he was in Southampton and I was in Birmingham and the broadcast was passed from one to the other. At the end of the day Brian's clock was a little bit ahead of mine but there was still radio time to be filled so he passed it over to me with the remark which has been all round the cricket world, 'We have just time for some more balls from Rex Alston.'

I will always have wonderful memories of Brian and Pauline. Typical of the man was his kindness and thoughtfulness. When I was in hospital having a knee operation some years ago, Brian phoned my wife every day for news. I shall miss his cheery voice on the telephone terribly.

Jonathan Agnew

'Aggers' will always be remembered for the moment he sent Johnners – and the whole nation besides – into hysterics by describing how Ian Botham had dislodged a bail 'just failing to get his leg over.'

This is an excerpt from their 'summary' during the England–West Indies Test at the Oval in 1991, by courtesy of the BBC.

JOHNNERS   Botham in the end out in the most extraordinary way.
AGGERS   Oh, it was ever so sad . . . it was interesting . . . we were talking and he had just started to loosen up, he had started to look, perhaps, for the big blows . . .

It was a bouncer and he tried to hook it. Why he tried to hook Ambrose I'm not sure because on this sort of pitch it's a very difficult prospect. It smacked him on the helmet, I think – I'm not quite sure where it actually hit him.

JOHNNERS Shoulder, I think.

AGGERS Shoulder, was it? As he tried to hook, he lost his balance . . . and he knew, this is the tragic thing about it, he knew exactly what was going to happen . . . he tried to step over the stumps and just flicked a bail with his right pad.

JOHNNERS He more or less tried to do the splits over it and, unfortunately, the inner part of his thigh must have just removed the bail.

AGGERS He just didn't quite get his leg over.

JOHNNERS Anyhow, he did very well indeed, batting one hundred and thirty-one minutes, and hit three fours; then we had Lewis playing extremely well for his forty-seven not out . . . Aggers, do stop it . . . and he was joined by DeFreitas, who— um— was in for forty minutes . . . useful little partnership there, they put on thirty-five in forty minutes . . . then . . . and he was caught by Dujon off Walsh. Lawrence, always entertaining, batted for thirty-five minutes (*starts laughing*) thirty-five minutes (*laughing even more*) hit a four over the wicket-keeper's h . . . (*dissolves into helpless laughter*) . . . Aggers, for goodness sake, stop it . . . he hit a f. . . (*complete collapse*).

AGGERS Yes . . . Lawrence, who had . . . (*dissolves into laughter as well*) . . . extremely well.

JOHNNERS (*In hysterics*) He hit a four over the wicket-keeper's head . . . (*continuing in a high-pitched, strangulated voice*) . . . and he was out for nine . . . and Tufnell came in . . . batted for twelve minutes, then was caught by Haynes off Patterson for two . . . and there were fifty-four extras and England were all out for four hundred and nineteen . . . I've stopped laughing now.

There was something unique about listening to Johnners burbling away in the commentary box. An English summer would not have been complete without his expressive description of a day at Lord's. Delivered with the cultured tones of an Upper Sixth Former, his inimitable style of commentating painted a vivid picture for the cricket enthusiast or the casual listener alike. His sense of humour, which one would associate with a member of the Lower Fourth rather than a man of eighty, was wickedly infectious.

'Fine delivery that,' I suggested to Trevor Bailey as Waqar Younis beat Mike Atherton outside the off stump at the Oval the year before last.

'Yes,' the Boil agreed sagely. 'It's remarkable how he can whip it out just before tea.'

An innocent comment which even failed to register a snort from the Bearded Wonder (Bill Frindall) sitting to my left and which must have passed way over the heads of 99 per cent of the audience. But not Johnners, who dissolved into a pitiful fit of giggles, making commentating on the next delivery a supreme effort.

It was not merely the launch which caused the problem. When Johnners started, his whole face seemed to explode. His eyes, normally hidden by those extraordinary drooping eyebrows, blinked furiously as tears streamed down his cheeks. He cast a helpless glance in your direction, begging for assistance, but speaking from more than one experience, it was at that point when one's own resistance broke down completely.

Sadly, he and I were banned from conducting the close of play summary together. Peter Baxter, *Test Match Special*'s producer, finally lost patience after another show-stopping performance at Lord's last summer. It was our first attempt since the infamous 'leg over' incident featuring Ian Botham at the Oval in 1991 and as such was keenly anticipated by myself but not so by Johnners who lapsed into convulsions the moment the plan was pencilled into our rota.

At first, we decided the only way we could possibly conduct the summary was for us both to sit at opposite ends of the commentary box and not look at each other. Johnners duly stuck himself away on the microphone to the extreme left, preparing himself for the ordeal, and appeared supremely confident until I sidled up and nestled in right beside him.

From that moment it was doomed. I'll hold up my hand and confess that I cracked first. But in my defence, can you really imagine Javed Miandad 'opening his legs up like a croquet hoop and tickling a ball down to fine leg'?

Johnners soldiered on bravely, aware that I had been rendered completely speechless, but then it became all too much and he had a giggling fit which resulted in a forty-second silence. During the ensuing may-hem, the electronic fault-detection system put a transmitter in the West Midlands off air and my Auntie in Hampstead dismantled her radio think-ing that the batteries had failed.

The door slamming behind us as Peter Baxter fled the commentary box in despair finally broke the silence.

It would be completely wrong, however, to look upon Johnners purely as an entertainer. Although *Test Match Special* does its best to disprove it, there are strict disciplines attached to radio.

One of the least popular aspects of the job is that someone has to be on the ground by five past eight in the morning for an early morning weather report and general chat on Radio 5 followed by the *Today* programme. Johnners devised the perfect plan which ensured that he would never be asked to do it again.

As usual, the producer's voice crackled in the headphones just before the sports bulletin began. 'Morning Brian. We've got a minute and a half with you, but it's to be very tight.

'You'll be asked three questions: What's the weather looking like, what did you think of yesterday's play, and what do you think will be a reasonable England total today. OK?'

'Fine,' replied Johnners, reaching for his stopwatch.

Sure enough, the presenter introduced Johnners, asking him how the weather looked. Johnners clicked his stopwatch and spoke for precisely ninety seconds, answering all three questions without them being asked by an increasingly irate presenter in the studio. A real pro – maybe I should attempt that next summer.

Above all, Johnners loved the game of cricket. I know that the controversies of the summer of 1992 depressed him terribly. He was commentating at Old Trafford during the distressing scenes involving Aqib Javed, Javed Miandad and Umpire Roy Palmer.

In the heat of the moment, Radio 5 joined Radio 3 and so Johnners had to recap on the events leading up to the fracas as well as simultaneously describing what was actually happening on the field. What happened was thirty seconds of pure magic.

I have heard that clip over and over again since that afternoon and have often wondered how I would have coped if it had all happened ten minutes earlier when I was in the hot seat.

I consider myself very fortunate to have had the chance of working with Johnners. Someone said to me that Johnners was the last of a dying breed. I know what they meant but the comment suggests that there must have been others in broadcasting like Johnners.

If that is the case, I have not heard them.

Trevor Bailey

'The Boil' and Johnners had at least one thing in common – their love of excruciating puns.

I became more than just an acquaintance of Brian Johnston when I was still playing Test cricket. Although the relationship between international players and the media was far more amicable in my era, Brian managed to maintain over the years his close links with the players because he was so genuine, dependable, amusing and the most gentle of critics. He loved cricket and cricketers.

Our acquaintanceship developed into friendship when Brian was sent by the BBC to cover an Australian tour and I was in the MCC party. On the long, carefree journey out by ship and in Australia we spent a considerable amount of time together as we possessed a similar sense of humour and an appreciation of the absurd. We both adored excruciating puns, Old Time Music Hall and jokes like:

'Hullo, hullo, 'ave you read Shakespeare?'

'No, but I've red socks.'

We saw our first duck-billed platypus together. Brian immediately and typically pointed out that the nasal equipment of the prehistoric creature had something in common with his own. This led naturally to whether the Johnstons would have been able to teach the Flintstones cricket.

Our friendship became closer when Brian left television to become a regular on *Test Match Special*, which I had joined as a summarizer several years earlier. The result was that I had the good fortune to spend some two decades with him broadcasting Test cricket, not only in this country, but also in Australia, the Caribbean and India. He was enormous fun to work with and throughout our long association there was never a cross word, which illustrates that he was a very, very tolerant individual. In addition to the hours we spent in each other's company, broadcasting and watching cricket, there were numerous trips and shows as well as countless breakfasts, cups of coffee, lunches, teas, dinners, chocolate cakes and the odd glass of champagne.

Test Match Special was already a well-established, successful and popular sports programme when Brian became a full-time member. The star was unquestionably John Arlott. With his carefully cultivated Hampshire brogue, splendid delivery and erudite phraseology, he was undoubtedly the best painter of word pictures the game has ever known. Brian brought to the show his own brand of humour and his own special style of relaxed broadcasting which made the listener feel that the events were being described for him by a close friend. He epitomized that favourite uncle, kind, gentle and amusing, with a permanent twinkle in his eye. Eventually Brian was to become the resident comedian and centrepiece of a show which appealed to many who were not especially interested in cricket.

John Arlott was probably right when he said that *Test Match Special* was a folk rather than a sports programme, especially when one remembers the number of listeners who have written in to say that they prefer it when it rains! Unquestionably the programme would never have achieved its listening figures if it had contented itself solely with describing what was happening out in the middle, which can be (and often is) boring for the spectator, but not for the listener if Brian was on the mike. During the summer of 1992 I was extolling the delights of India to Brian in the commentary box at Lord's. He mentioned that it was one of the few places where he had never broadcast a Test and how he would like to do one. I suggested that he and his wife Pauline should join my small party which I was taking for *The Cricketer* to see the Tests in India that winter. Although Brian was eighty years old his concern had nothing to do with the long flight or the travel. It was the food.

It was not that he did not enjoy food but it had to be plain and simple.

He could not face the culinary delights of Europe with their very special sauces which captivate my own taste buds, so, clearly, the many Indian and Chinese delights to be had in Asia were not for him. Fortunately, these days all the big Indian hotels have one restaurant able to accommodate the needs of the most delicate of stomachs, with the result that I was able to persuade Brian and Pauline to go with me to India. He enjoyed the cricket (and the atmosphere) enormously, especially as most of the bowling was done by spinners, while I shall always treasure the sight of the waiter in Goa cycling to Brian's apartment with his English breakfast held aloft with one hand. Quite apart from the obvious pleasure of having him with us on this trip, fate provided us with one classic example of his charm. Delhi airport is not a place I would recommend to be stranded. My party arrived there at about 7 a.m. after a very early morning call at our hotel. Smog accounted for the initial delay but a complete absence of information, an acute shortage of refreshments and a lack of seats did make our seven-hour delay pass rather slowly. But it never even ruffled Brian's composure and helped to explain why he was so universally popular. He treated everybody the same and was prepared to talk to anybody, even if it was inconvenient.

Brian loved people and he enjoyed talking to them, which was one of the reasons he became such an accomplished after-dinner speaker. A natural chatterbox, he was also a true professional, as well as being a charitable man without malice, who never quite grew up and still relished the jokes and japes of his days at Eton. Yet he had won the Military Cross with the Guards and they do not give those away lightly. It will never be quite the same again for me to go into the commentary box at Lord's and not to be greeted by, 'Hullo Boilers, have you heard the one about?' But thanks for the memory.

Tony Lewis

Former England captain and now TV anchorman Tony Lewis felt it was a privilege to work with Johnners.

Brian Johnston was a spontaneous broadcaster whose touch was felicitous because he was a good man with generous thoughts. One day he looked at the commentators' rota in a Test match, saw my initials and simply announced that the next commentator would be ARL. I have been 'ARL' to many ever since.

'Oh, dear,' he later broadcast, 'Mrs Lewis is not very keen on her husband being called ARL and I would love to help her but I fear it is too late . . . in any case, I think ARL suits him rather well.'

In fact, Brian did have a wit for naming, schoolboy in style but affectionate. Peter Baxter was Backers, Henry Blofeld was Blowers, and Don Mosey was The Alderman, but for John Arlott it was usually John Arlott. There was a high regard between Arlott and Johnners and neither trampled on the other's professional space. It was a huge privilege to work on the same team as them, both confident in their crafts.

Johnners, of course, reached heights of humour and fun which transcended the most serious moments and persuaded us all that cricket, when all was said, was but a game to be enjoyed. He was hurt by bad behaviour both on and off the field. Life's game should be played with courtesy and a certain decorum according to principles of behaviour which would suit in any walk of life.

Listening to Brian broadcast cricket when I was at home or in a car was to be allowed to sit next to him at the game. He gave you the feeling of being the intimate eavesdropper. You had joined his company, joined his picnic and met the friends he had brought along with him. With Brian you had a day out at the match even though you were ill in bed, perhaps, or digging holes in the road.

I remember his last months so vividly because he and Pauline visited an England Test series in India for the first time. He loved it: took it all in his stride. A man vastly experienced by many vicissitudes, he was absolutely certain that the life he had chosen was the one which suited his talents best.

And he swam up and down the pool in the Taj Mahal Hotel in Bombay and looked as if he could keep going for ever. I suppose his presence on *Test Match Special* had become wonderfully eternal in this life so short and so we will miss him and talk about him for as long as we are able.

Don Mosey

There were some fierce encounters when 'The Alderman' and Johnners shared the same commentary box, though they had nothing to do with cricket.

For eighteen summers Brian and I played a pencil-and-paper word game which had its origin (I always suspected) in those teenage Johnstonian years spent in the offices of the family business in London.

It was basically simple and provided us with literally hours of entertainment. We each drew a grid of twenty-five linked squares on a piece of paper and then in turn nominated an individual letter which had to be entered in one of the squares by *both* players. The object was to build up words. We scored ten points for a five-letter word, five points for a four-letter word, one point for a three-letter word.

Over the years I calculated we played nearly 4,000 games of which Brian won by far the most, but he did so by tactics which used to drive me into a frenzy. He tried to build up the same words in every game and as two of his favourite words were 'TRUSS' and 'SEWER', I used to explode with exasperation. 'There's got to be something bent about a chap who habitually uses words like that.'

It scarcely needs to be said that this delighted Brian hugely. Most listeners to *Test Match Special* would be well aware of the results because Brian took delight in announcing them at regular intervals. Gradually, other members of the commentary team took it upon themselves to make similar announcements. 'Oh dear, The Alderman has lost yet another game.'

As well as building up one's own words, each player had, of course, to try to confound the opponent by slipping in letters which were not expected. Occasionally, very rarely, I could win what turned out to be a very low-scoring game. Even more rarely, there was an argument about the validity of one of our words. This was usually Brian arguing that one of *mine* was unacceptable because, as I have said, he tried always to work in his own . . . Truss, Sewer, Stars and one or two others. I knew very well indeed his winning formulae but was not able to counter them very often. He once argued that my word 'SEPTS' was unacceptable and so fierce a debate ensued that Brian put it to the nation, so to speak, by quoting the word to listeners.

I am delighted to report that B.J.'s large daily postbag was swelled even further during the next few days with letters telling him that not only was a sept a fence or enclosure but also a sub-division of a Scottish or Irish clan. It thus could legitimately be pluralized into SEPTS. So I won that argument, if not the series. It was my job (simply because Brian decreed it!) to keep the score throughout a season and it usually ended something like 125–76 in his favour. These results were announced by my delighted opponent during the final Test of the year, and sometimes during the Gillette (later NatWest) Cup Final. On those occasions it was virtually impossible to insert such an irrelevance amidst all the excitement but somehow he managed it.

I never knew whether these sessions had a similar effect on B.J. but I do know that I went to bed on many nights with five-letter words flashing through my drowsy mind, usually words like Truss and Sewer. And I once spent a complete fortnight on a beach in Brittany practising with my wife for the next encounter with Brian. There was no need for pencil and paper – we covered acres of sand on a deserted beach!

Vic Marks

A relative newcomer to the Test Match Special *team, 'Skid' Marks could not help but admire Brian's professionalism.*

Behind all the japes and chocolate cakes Johnners was a consummate professional. Whenever I was in the box at a home Test match, I made the point of listening in to his interview in the 'View from the Boundary' slot. He was a master at relaxing his subjects. I'm sure he could have eked out from John Major any likely tax rises faster than a Paxman or a Dimbleby.

At the Lord's Test of 1992 (I think) he had prepared to interview Ned Sherrin. But this time the presenter in Broadcasting House announced: 'And now back to Lord's for "A View from the Boundary" with Ned Sherrin.' The tables had been surreptitiously turned by producer, Peter Baxter, and Johnners himself was to be interviewed.

I watched him closely. He blinked, gulped for half a second, uttered a brief, 'Oh, no,' and then proceeded to give, rather than conduct, the perfect interview. So calm was his reaction that we wondered whether he had uncovered Baxter's secret. He hadn't, but his instinct to ensure that the show goes on without a hitch took over.

On another occasion, at Headingley 1993, *Test Match Special* was being broadcast on Radio 5 and started with a jingle during which Jon Agnew would deliver a soundbite in up-beat style, presumably to whet the listeners' appetite – not the Radio 3 format at all.

An elaborate hoax was engineered in which Agnew made a desperate phone call saying he had been unavoidably detained; this ensured that Johnners had the 'disc jockey' role. Peter Baxter did his best to prolong the agony by making Johnners have several practice runs – 'Sorry Johnners. That was one second too long.' – 'Could you just raise your voice at the end?'

The whole ruse worked perfectly as Agnew finally guffawed into the box – except that Johnners had followed his instructions so immaculately that he might have been considered as a replacement for Dave Lee Travis on Radio 1.

Brian Johnston getting to grips with the microphone during his early days at the BBC (*Radio Times Picture Library*).

Johnners the stuntman in his 'Let's Go Somewhere' feature during *In Town Tonight:* commentating while 'Mad Johnny' Davies and the Motor-cycle Maniacs leapt over his head (*Syndication International*)...

...finding out what it was like to be attacked by a police Alsatian (*BBC*)...

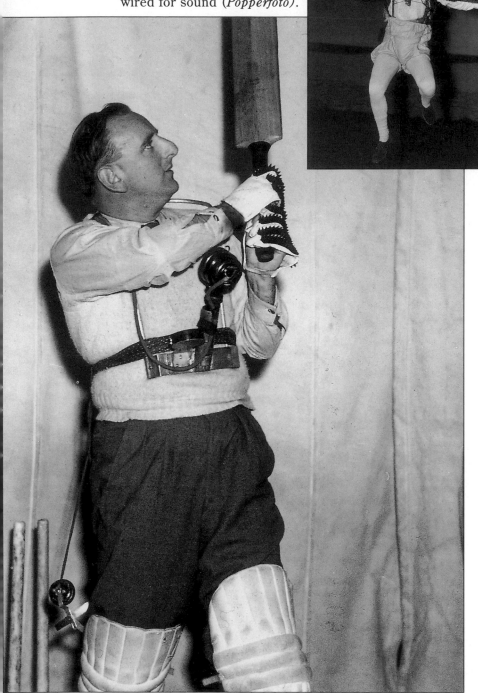

...rehearsing for 'the flying ballet'
(*Syndication International*)...

...hitting out in the cricket nets while
wired for sound (*Popperfoto*).

BJ the commentator showing his versatility: describing the Coronation procession from Hyde Park with Bernard Braden in 1953 (*BBC*)...

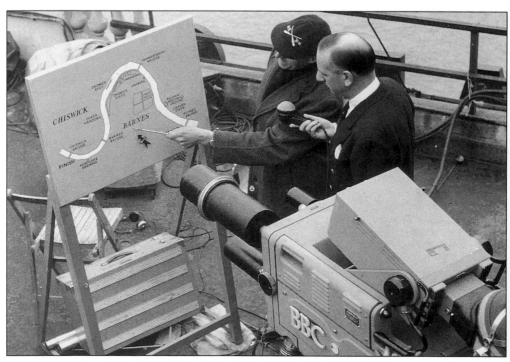

...studying a plan of the Boat Race course with former Oxford Blue Edgar Tomlin in 1956 (*BBC*)...

...pioneering cricket on television with E.W. (Jim) Swanton and
Peter West in 1953 (*BBC*)...

...and commentating from his beloved Lord's in 1957 (*BBC*).

Brian presenting awards to local cricketers at Wombwell Cricket Lovers' Society in 1958 *(Wombwell Cricket Lovers' Society)*.

BJ addresses the Lord's Taverners at the Eve of Test dinner *(The Lord's Taverners)*.

Brian with one of 'his boys' from the Metropolitan Sports and Social Club for the Visually Handicapped (*Metropolitan Sports and Social Club*).

Down Your Way visits the Wiltshire village of Lacock – BJ with producer Anthony Smith and audio supervisor Brian Martin (*BBC*).

Tony Cozier

Tony Cozier, the doyen of West Indian cricket commentators, has another particular claim to fame. Even Johnners could not dream up a nickname for him.

It never took Brian Johnston very long to indulge his penchant for practical jokes and puns.

The first full series in which I shared the commentary box was England's tour of the Caribbean under Colin Cowdrey in 1968 – and I was soon the victim of the pranks which I was to become all too familiar with down the passing years. It was the first Test at the Queen's Park Oval in Port of Spain, one of those grounds that is a nightmare for those of us who also write for the Press with the radio commentary box and the press box at opposite ends of the ground. The route to and fro involved either a stroll around the boundary to the catcalls and heckling of the ground crowd, upset at any one of a thousand things that might have appeared under your name in the morning's newspapers, or a longer, more cowardly detour along the streets outside.

On the day in question, the way was easier. It had been raining, there was no play and I took the chance of the straightest possible line between my two workplaces, across the field itself, from press to commentary box. I arrived to find, to my surprise, the 'on air' light illuminated and Brian chatting away on the microphone. I hadn't time to sit down when he announced my arrival and advised listeners that I would take over immediately and reveal to them the statistics of the tour so far.

Taken aback, I took my seat next to him and tried to babble my way out of it, starting with the prospects of play. Johnners would have none of it. 'I've promised listeners you'll fill them in on the statistical details as we've had some calls asking for them,' he said. The next few seconds were sheer panic as I pressed in vain for something, anything, from our scorer, fumbled in my bag for the morning's *Trinidad Guardian* which did have a few details, and generally lost my cool while trying to sound intelligible.

What was a few minutes felt like hours until Johnners, beaming all over

Bill Tidy

his face, burst into laughter with everyone else in the box. We weren't on the air at all and I'd raised my blood pressure for nothing!

A few nights later, having forgiven and forgotten, we were together at the bar of the Queen's Park Hotel before heading to the dining room when a mutual friend, an English journalist covering the tour, came over to join us with one of those stunningly beautiful girls for which Trinidad is famous on his arm.

Obviously, and understandably, proud of his conquest and eager to show off, he introduced her: 'Johnners, I'd like you to meet Annette,' he beamed.

'Oh,' Johnners replied in a flash. 'You know when you told me the other day you'd had a net, I thought you meant you'd been to cricket practice!'

Like all of us who were the butt of Johnners' jokes and wisecracks, the journo with the deflated ego simply had a good laugh. Johnners was always so full of fun, always conscious of seeing the happy side of life and the best in people. He would have been crestfallen if anyone took offence at his sense of humour. They seldom ever did. But you always had to be on your guard for his latest prank!

Neville Oliver

No trouble with this one! When this genial Tasmanian first arrived in England, Johnners promptly christened him 'Doctor', as Neville explains . . .

At the end of the Ashes Test at the Oval in 1993 I said my farewell to Brian Johnston. The conversation dealt briefly with the wonderful summer of friendship that we had again enjoyed in the *Test Match Special* box but in much more detail with Johnners' plans for the next eighteen months. 'Possibly see you at the Durban Test, Doctor, then off to Barbados and Antigua on a cruise to see the last couple of England versus the West Indies Tests, a summer at home and then to Australia to see the 94/95 Ashes battle.'

Brian Johnston may have been eighty-one by the measure of a birth certificate but to me he never really got past thirty in his zest for life. Not for Johnners the feet-up contemplation of the aged when there was so much to see and do.

In the *Test Match Special* box some name other than your own is seen as a necessity. 'Bearders,' 'Jenkers,' 'Backers,' are the standard modes of greeting for Bill Frindall, Christopher Martin-Jenkins and Peter Baxter. In 1989, on my first Ashes Tour to England, Johnners said, 'I shall call you the Doctor,' (Neville Oliver = N.O. = Doctor No, the James Bond character). From then on I was greeted with 'Morning Doctor,' or 'Your next commentator will be the Doctor.'

Imagine then the glee that came from Brian when a Scottish doctor, at the end of the 1993 tour, wrote to me offering a locum at his practice for a month. I can still hear Brian's roar of appreciation.

I will never believe that life for Johnners was ever vaguely meant to be a burden. He told me, with growing enthusiasm, about the total futility of one of his major tasks during the Second World War. Mounted in a side-car he patrolled the cliffs of Dover with the order that, if he spotted any Germans in the vicinity, he was to execute a U-turn and report their presence to Headquarters. Years later he would remark to me that as the defender of the cliffs he didn't really believe the idea was workable. It would have been a great sight, though!

During the presentation of cheques and medallions at the end of a 1993 Ashes Test we received the list of people who would be in the official party on the balcony. Jon Agnew discussed with me the addition of a name, grabbed a typewriter, inserted the addition, then photocopied the document to make the change less obvious and handed the sheet to the man responsible for broadcasting the ceremony about to take place – Brian Johnston. This was to be our most impressive practical joke of the summer. Johnners read down the list and at the bottom proudly read that the Managing Director of the Cornhill Insurance Group, Mr Hugh Jarse, was present. What a roar went up in the box – how well Johnners took it. It was a rarity to catch the practical joker so perfectly.

Brian always seemed indestructible. I was stunned to hear of his heart attack. I was devastated by his passing. My father had passed away twenty years before and somehow the death of Brian left me with a similar feeling of loss.

It was a privilege to have known him and the cricket commentary boxes will never be quite the same without him.

Alan Richards

'Sir Alan,' as Brian called him, was soon put at ease on his arrival from New Zealand.

In 1973 I became the first radio cricket commentator to accompany a New Zealand touring team to England. *Test Match Special* had been in existence then for three years.

Although not altogether inexperienced, I faced the prospect of working alongside such household names as Brian Johnston, John Arlott, Christopher Martin-Jenkins, Trevor Bailey, Fred Trueman and others with some trepidation. But I need not have worried. The Kiwis' opening match was at Worcester and when Brian Johnston joined me to cover the game for *Sport on Two* I was quickly put at ease by his friendliness.

The same warm welcome subsequently awaited me in the *Test Match Special* commentary box where I soon noticed how Brian's vivacity was instrumental in welding a group of strong individual personalities into a superb team of entertainers.

A visiting commentator from Australia or New Zealand is always conscious of the need to feed additional background information to his listeners at home. After all, most of them are sacrificing precious sleep as they lie in bed with their radios. So, normally every minute of one's commentary stint is fully utilized.

However, at Headingley in 1983 New Zealand listeners might have wondered whether I had dozed off early in my commentary period!

Certainly I contributed to the débâcle which occurred but Johnners, as usual, was the main culprit.

The previous evening the entire *Test Match Special* team had attended the launching of Bob Willis's new book, *The Captain's Diary*, an event of which I was reminded when I noticed Don Mosey deposit his now-unwanted invitation to the function in the commentary-box trashcan nearby. Wishing to help publicize the book I mentioned our attendance at the launch but, unable to recall the title with certainty, I added, 'The name of Bob's new book escapes me just for the moment. However, I'll be able to tell you when I've delved into the rubbish bin here . . .'

I got no further as Brian Johnston immediately dissolved into hysterical laughter, quickly followed by everyone else in the box. Realizing my gaffe and involuntarily caught up in the pervading air of hilarity, I struggled to regain my composure. Suddenly I became aware that an over was about to commence. The bowler was starting his approach.

Looking anxiously around, I discovered that all the other commentators, similarly affected by Brian's uninhibited laughter, had now vacated their microphones. I was completely on my own, with millions of listeners in England and abroad. But having seen B.J. doubled up at the back of the box, I found myself unequal to the challenge. I opened my mouth but I was still shaking too violently to speak.

In all my commentary experience before and since, I have never missed describing a couple of deliveries as I did on that day at Headingley. It was a quite dreadful experience over which I had absolutely no control. I imagine the effects of laughing gas are somewhat similar.

When I mentioned the feeling of total helplessness to Brian later he replied, 'Don't worry, Sir Alan [the nickname he bestowed on me]. It was all jolly good fun!' And Bob Willis told me later it was the best publicity his book could possibly have received!

In most other broadcasting boxes a similar slip of the tongue may have brought forth a few suppressed sniggers. But in the *Test Match Special* box Johnners rarely missed an opportunity to create a hilarious situation, which was one of the main reasons his colleagues enjoyed their *Test Match Special* experience so much.

Throughout each of my five tours to England, Brian Johnston's ready wit and irrepressible sense of fun were always in evidence. His quite brilliant interviews during the lunch interval also revealed his high intelligence and wide general knowledge. But, above all, my enduring memory of Brian is of the warm hand of friendship he extended so readily on my first visit to England in 1973.

Ali Bacher

Charles Fortune, Brian's legendary South African contemporary, has not been in the best of health so Dr Ali Bacher, former Test captain turned administrator, pays this tribute.

Although not of my era, Brian Johnston was known to me as a legendary personality. It is sad that he is not with us to celebrate South Africa's return to international competition having seen us go into the 'wilderness'. He was a true friend of South African cricket and paid several visits to our country, where he made many friends and is remembered for his genial personality and, of course, his wonderful cricket commentaries. One of his closest friends in South Africa, the equally legendary Charles Fortune, has spoken of Brian on many occasions.

Broadcasting is indeed a gift and one which Brian possessed. He brought the game to thousands of cricket lovers who could not be at the ground, in a voice that was familiar and popular with BBC listeners. In the days before we had television every move that was made on the field had to be brought alive by the commentator. That he did with tremendous flair. He was wonderful – his knowledge and love of cricket plus his great sense of humour and *joie de vivre* exuded his enjoyment of the game and gave added pleasure for thousands of listeners.

We pay tribute to Brian as a lover of the game and a loyal friend of South African cricket.

7

BEHIND THE TIMBERS

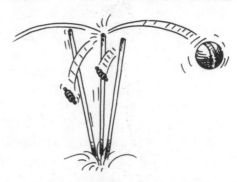

Cricket was, of course, Brian's first love and from his early days at his preparatory school he always kept wicket, probably, he once explained, because he thought the hard ball would not hurt so much if he wore gloves.

His greatest disappointment was his failure to get into the Eton XI to play Harrow at Lord's, but he did captain the school 2nd XI, played for his college at Oxford and went on to play for clubs like I Zingari, the Butterflies, Oxford University Authentics and, most of all, Eton Ramblers.

After the war he played for the MCC and the BBC as well as turning out in a large number of charity games with a host of stars from the worlds of sport and entertainment.

Godfrey Evans

Godfrey Evans, the inimitable Kent and England wicket-keeper, was naturally one of Brian's idols.

Whenever I played with Brian, he would come breezing into the dressing-room and say, 'Godders, you don't have to worry about missing anything behind the timbers today. I'll be there not you, my dear boy, and I'll be taking your leg-spinners.'

And I would say, 'Johnners, can you read my googly? Don't forget I bowl flight, spin and gin!'

He wasn't a bad wicket-keeper, very keen and enthusiastic as you would expect, but I remember him best for the chances he missed – which he obviously did occasionally.

He would laugh and make such a song and dance about it that he'd immediately have everyone else falling about in fits of laughter as well. The missed chance was instantly forgotten as we all looked forward to him missing another one!

His batting was not quite as memorable. He used to try but he didn't really hit the ball very hard and was more of a sticker than anything else. I don't think he minded if he didn't bat at all as long as he could keep wicket.

Wicket-keeping fascinated him and though I don't remember him ever asking me for any advice on the field he always wanted plenty off it. He wanted to be able to express a correct opinion when he was commentating and would often ask me what I thought about different wicket-keepers and how they kept. Take Alec Stewart, for instance. When he takes a ball wide of the off stump or the leg stump he nearly always falls over and Brian wanted to know why. I explained that it's because he doesn't get his feet in the right position. He should try to cut the ball off more by moving in an arc with the bowler. That way he would get much closer to it and stay on his feet more.

Johnners loved hearing about things like that, even the more obscure things that most observers wouldn't notice. I used to tuck the little finger of my right hand under the left hand and he'd ask, 'Why do you do that?' I used to do it because when there was a very high ball swirling in the sky it was very difficult to judge the exact position with your head right back and I wanted to keep the gloves together so that the ball didn't go through them.

The only one I remember dropping was off Alec Bedser on the 1950–51 tour of Australia under Freddie Brown. I got right underneath it and started falling backwards as it drifted in the wind, with the result that it hit me in the chest instead of the gloves. I don't remember too many people falling about in fits of laughter at the time but it didn't really matter. Ian Johnson hit the very next ball straight down Brian Close's throat.

Talking of Alec Bedser, Johnners used to love to see me standing up to him and would chide Alan Knott for standing back to medium-pacers like Basil d'Oliveira and Bob Woolmer. 'Even if the ball hit the stumps,' he'd scoff, 'it wouldn't knock the bails off.'

He was only joking, of course, like he always was – and my abiding memory of him will be of the way he greeted me in recent years when I was working with Ladbrokes and used to take the latest betting up to the commentary box.

'Ah,' he would cry, 'here comes Godders with the odders from Ladders!'

Doug Insole

Doug Insole, the former Essex and England batsman and now a leading administrator, analyses the Johnners style.

Brian Johnston was always modest about his ability as a cricketer. And justifiably so. I am not too sure at what age he would reckon that he was in his prime but I suspect that I must have missed it.

I played quite a few games with him in the 1950s for the Lord's Taverners and, I remember vaguely, for one or two other 'Select XIs', and his performances behind what he almost always referred to as 'the timbers' were usually an entertainment in themselves. Johnners had the sharp features of Godfrey Evans, and I believe that he sometimes borrowed the maestro's inner gloves, but I am struggling to find any additional points of similarity.

Johnners liked to look efficient down the legside. His foot movements would take him smoothly – in the style of Victor Sylvester, to whom he sometimes referred – outside the line of the leg stump but his hands somehow seemed to get left behind. I do recall, however, a specific occasion on which he enjoyed a sweet moment of triumph.

I think the match was played at Harlow and I believe that the Taverners were involved. I may be wrong on both counts, but it matters not. What matters is that the batsman had danced down the pitch to our spinner and had missed the ball which turned and missed the leg stump. Johnners was in position, *à la* ballroom dancing manual, and, despite snatching at it, he had the ball securely in his gloves with the batsman stranded down the pitch. He made to whip off the bails but was inhibited by the fact that while the 'finger' end of his gloves had grabbed the ball, the 'wrist' end of his gloves had grabbed his shirt. He made a couple of hilariously abortive attempts to take the ball to the wicket but seemed to be fearful that if he opened his gloves at the back to free his shirt, he would relinquish his hold on the ball.

Watching this pantomime from a distance was the batsman who, on seeing Johnners take the ball, had given up the ghost. He now saw a glimmer of hope and made a belated attempt to get back to his crease. He was foiled, however, by our hero who decided to launch himself full length at the wicket, gloves foremost. With a yell of unrestrained glee, he flattened all three stumps while letting go a stentorian appeal which was, after due and solemn consideration, upheld by the umpire.

It was very shortly after this incident that the aforementioned and much revered T.G. Evans pioneered the wearing by wicket-keepers of a tight-fitting shirt in order to avoid any possible recurrence of the misfortune so nearly experienced by his disciple, one B.A. Johnston.

Tributes to Brian have emphasized, quiet correctly, how popular he was amongst the cricketing fraternity. He was a kind man and he was very supportive, in the most positive way, of people involved in the game. In the fortnight or so immediately prior to his heart attack, I was on the bill with him at a benefit dinner for Harry Brind at the Oval, and I sat alongside him at a lunch at the Hilton to celebrate Reg Hayter's eightieth birthday.

At the Oval, he trotted out a broadly based selection of his music hall gags, spiced with a few gems from the commentary box, and ended with a delightful tribute to the importance of Harry Brind's work as 'pitches supremo'; while at the Hilton he was honouring a media colleague of very long standing for whom he had a genuine affection. He was under no obligation to be at either function and, in the middle of a taxing schedule of stage engagements, it was typical of Brian that he should make such a tremendous effort.

I spent a bit of time with him in the winter of 1992–93 in Goa during England's tour of India and one evening we had dinner together at a beach restaurant attached to the hotel at which he was staying.

'What do you reckon to the lamb cutlets, Johnners?' I asked.

'Probably goat, Inners,' he said, 'but it's the nearest we're going to get to a sheep in this part of the world so I suggest we take a chance.'

We came to no harm and Brian survived to tell the tale in *Test Match Special* last summer. That he will not be doing so again must be a matter of the deepest regret to anybody and everybody that enjoys cricket.

Sir Colin Cowdrey

Sir Colin Cowdrey, the Kent and England captain who became chairman of the International Cricket Council, will never forget meeting Brian for the first time.

The first time I met Brian Johnston was in the Kent dressing room at Lord's in the early fifties. I had come to know his voice really well as a regular listener to *In Town Tonight* and through his early cricket radio commentaries. It was quite an excitement to me when the door burst open, the bugle call for which he was famous sounded, and the voice was ringing around the dressing room. 'Hello Godders,' for he and Godfrey Evans had become good fun companions around the Test matches.

Godfrey introduced him to the rest of the players and by chance there were two other great wicket-keepers on the balcony, Leslie Ames and

Hopper Levett. You can imagine the noise and the chatter of gossip that ensued.

Hopper challenged Johnston with, 'You keep telling us on the radio how well you're playing yourself – what do you do?'

Feigning mock horror, back came the retort, 'You haven't heard about me – good heavens – I'm a Master behind the timbers,' going through the motions with his two hands together stumping and catching. I had never heard the words 'behind the timbers' before denoting wicket-keeping and it rather tickled me. With very quick movements he was wafting his hands about, 'If I'd kept wicket to Tich Freeman I would have trapped the victims just like Leslie and Hopper did, and I'd have stood up to Alec Bedser and been even sharper down the leg side than Godfrey Evans, and made less noise about it.'

'I can see you're keen, Johnners, but your hand action is dreadful – we've got to put that right,' said Godfrey stirring it up. 'And your feet don't move,' chimed Leslie Ames. 'And don't you ever move your body at all?' came Hopper Levett. 'Looks a hopeless case I think, boys,' said Godfrey. 'It'll need all next winter's training – no chance of a miracle with a technique like yours I'm afraid, Johnners.'

'Well, charming to meet such gracious and encouraging Kent Hoppers. You've really lifted my game, and I'll keep you posted with my progress.'

The Kent team had loved the little sideshow, typical of the fun and camaraderie of a cricket dressing room. As he walked by me on the way out he said, 'Good luck young Cowders – if you can break through to the top with all these ruffians around, you will have my admiration.' Just before he went out of the dressing-room door he turned and gave me a huge wink for good luck, 'You'll do it, I know you will, we're all behind you. Good luck.'

I was very touched. I shall never forget it.

M.J.K. Smith

Universally known by his initials, Warwickshire's M.J.K. (Mike) Smith is another former Test captain who also played international rugby and wrote this tribute while managing the England cricket team in the West Indies.

The cartoon, which I believe appeared in *Private Eye*, of Brian knocking on the Pearly Gates and asking, 'Is Godders in?' perfectly captured the image of the man. An image, I am sure, he would be entirely relaxed about, light-hearted to the end as he was.

It is well known that Brian's two major interests were cricket and the theatre. It wasn't that he was theatrical in his commentaries, but he had a style which flowed and flourished and also added to the attraction of the play. People go to the theatre to be entertained and to enjoy themselves. Brian felt exactly the same way about a visit to the cricket, a game he truly loved, the more so played in the right manner with panache and style.

The easiest man in the world to get to know and like, it followed that the players he found most interesting were those whom he saw as entertainers; players with flair. It helped that his career in broadcasting commenced with Denis Compton in full flow. Denis was then the Brylcream Boy, debonair and dashing, the man at centre stage playing the Noel Coward lead.

We shall miss Brian, but at least we know Godders will have good company.

Alec Stewart

Captain of Surrey and sometimes England, Alec Stewart belongs to a new generation of cricketers but soon fell under the Johnners spell.

I come from a cricketing family and I have been fascinated by the game for as long as I can remember. So, even when I was in the classroom at school, I was always desperate to know how the Test match was going. This is where Brian came in.

My trick was to wear a secret earpiece and thread the wire inside my sleeve to the mini radio in my pocket. Instead of learning about square roots and Shakespeare, I would be listening intently to Brian and John Arlott broadcasting the latest news from Lord's.

Once, though, I was rumbled. 'Stewart,' said the teacher, 'would you care to answer the question I have just asked?' Of course, I didn't have a clue what the question was and, as the teacher approached, he caught sight of the earpiece. He guessed immediately what I was doing.

'OK then, Stewart, if you can't answer that question, why don't you tell us if England are all out yet.' I'd got away with it, and my only punishment was to inform the rest of the class the latest score.

Subsequently, of course, I met Brian many times. He was always cheerful, always friendly – in fact, exactly the same away from the microphone as he was in front of it.

He presented me with a jeroboam of bubbly for winning the champagne moment at the first Test against Pakistan at Edgbaston in 1992, when I managed to score 190. I still have it as a permanent reminder of Johnners and will drink it only on a very special occasion.

Somehow, I always felt Johnners was a closet Surrey fan. You just had to look at his shoes to see why. He always wore chocolate and white co-respondent's shoes to Test matches and all that chocolate gave me the feeling he had a soft spot for the Oval. Chocolate, of course, is the colour of Surrey's cap.

In his younger days, Brian was a very enthusiastic wicket-keeper and, as I wear the gloves quite regularly, we would chat about life behind the stumps. One of Brian's little hobby horses was that 'keepers rarely stand up to medium-pacers these days. He used to tell me about how Godfrey Evans used to be up to the stumps to the bowling of Alec Bedser (after whom I was named, incidentally). But I must confess I resisted all Brian's attempts to persuade me to stand up to Waqar Younis.

8

BEYOND THE BOUNDARY

Brian Johnston was held in great affection far beyond the worlds of cricket and show business. Here are just three of them.

The Rt. Hon. John Major

Brian Johnston was, quite simply, unique. A national institution. For the many cricket lovers in the country, summers will not be the same without him.

He was part of my cricketing world from my youth. Little did I realize then that one day I would have the pleasure of joining him in commentary boxes at Test match grounds the length and breadth of the country.

Brian's association with cricket commentary began in 1946 and he distinguished himself in television before moving to radio in 1970. This was a medium he made his own. Remarkably, he retired officially in 1972 to enjoy one of the most active and entertaining retirements ever seen.

Paul Russell from Test Match Special 3 *(Queen Anne Press)*

Irrepressible and irreplaceable, Brian had the gift of communicating fun even at the dullest of matches. He had a schoolboy sense of humour but it was none the less amusing for that.

Famous for his prankster activities, one above all others comes to my mind. As ever, chocolate cake had a part to play. Having received yet another cake, Brian was engaged in passing pieces to his colleagues when Alan McGilvray came into the box to prepare for his stint. Brian passed a piece of particularly gooey confection to him. As soon as he had taken a giant mouthful Brian asked him what he thought of the ball that had just been bowled. A stunned McGilvray choked and uttered a few barely audible words while the rest of the team collapsed in helpless laughter.

Brian was also the master of inadvertent humour. Who could forget his description of Fred Titmus turning his arm over with the further comment that he had 'two short legs – one of them square'?

For my part I shall treasure those memories of the commentary box. There was never any of the sense of tension that normally prevails with the electronic media; it was more like visiting an old friend at home for afternoon tea.

If some were to say that I am a *Test Match Special* 'groupie' I freely confess to being so. Indeed I even took the opportunity of a live radio link in Barcelona in 1992 – where I was visiting the Olympic Games – to check on progress at a Test. If you can't actually be there then surely there is nothing better than sitting in the sun talking to Brian about the latest score.

Brian was, however, much more than just a cricket commentator. He took part in many programmes, perhaps most notably in fifteen years of *Down Your Way*. Aside from the pleasure of the programme, it is worth recording that while he could have carried on for many years he stopped at 733 editions. This equalled the record set by his predecessor, the outstanding Franklin Engelmann. It was absolutely typical of his gentlemanly approach that he would not seek to outdo one for whom he had such great respect.

As I pen this tribute to Brian I have not of course had the opportunity to read what else is written about him in this book. But I am utterly confident that what will shine through will be enormous warmth and affection for the man. All who listened to Brian felt they knew him well and that he was talking not to a wide audience but just to us as individuals, bringing the great game to us wherever we were.

Brian had a great gift and he shared it generously with all of us. I often wondered if there was a particular secret to his success and what his reply would have been. I can only guess but I would not have been surprised if it was, 'Oh, it's a piece of cake really.'

George Shearing

————

One of the most popular features of Test Match Special *was 'View from the Boundary' on Saturday lunchtimes when Brian would invite well-known personalities from all walks of life to chat about themselves and cricket. He particularly enjoyed his interview with the famous blind pianist George Shearing – and so did his guest.*

To meet Brian Johnston was to know Brian Johnston. I first met him in 1946 but it was forty-four years before we met again when I appeared on 'A View from the Boundary'. He had the uncanny ability to make me feel as if I were speaking to an old friend even though it was our first meeting for almost half a century. I was so impressed with the rapport between us that I was determined to invite the Johnstons to my next concert.

I did just that and asked them if they would like to join my wife and me for a late supper in our suite at the Berkeley following the show. Not only did they accept but they also waited patiently at the hotel while I attended to autographs and a bit of last-minute business at the theatre.

The next summer, when we returned to England, Polly and Brian invited us to lunch at their home. After lunch, we all went on to Lord's to watch a cricket match between blind players from London and Birmingham. Brian sat on my left and gave me a complete description of the game. That commentary for me was as professional as if he were commentating on a Test match to millions of listeners.

Brian also got me interested in membership in the Primary Club . . . a club very supportive of cricket as played by the blind.

I have known Brian Johnston for approximately four years and it feels as comfortable as if I had known him ten times that length. I shall miss him very much for as many years as I have left to live.

This is the interview, reproduced from Brian's book, More Views from the Boundary *(Methuen London, 1993), reprinted by permission of Reed Consumer Books.*

One of the bonuses of my 47 years of cricket commentary has been the way it has brought me in close touch with the blind. From our letters we know that we have thousands of blind listeners, who rely on the radio cricket commentator to paint the picture of a match for them. Many of them follow the placings and movements of fielders on a braille pattern of a cricket field. Some, like our special friend Mike Howell up at Old Trafford, actually come to Tests, and listen in to our commentaries. They like to feel that they are part of the crowd and enjoy absorbing the excitement and atmosphere of everything happening at the ground.

You can imagine therefore how pleased I was to receive a letter from a lady in Stow-on-the-Wold telling me that the world-famous blind pianist George Shearing came and lived there every summer, which he spent listening to *Test Match Special*. We immediately contacted him in New York and invited him to the first of the two Lord's Tests in 1990. MCC gave special permission for his wife, Elly, to accompany him up to our box in the pavilion – a privilege only those ladies who *work* in the pavilion enjoy.

I had met him just once, 44 years before during a broadcast from a restaurant off Bond Street. I had forgotten what a wonderful sense of humour he possessed and from the moment he entered the box he had us all laughing. Two years later I went at *his* invitation, to hear him in a concert at the Festival Hall. He gave a marvellous performance and I was fascinated to watch his fingers moving swiftly across the keyboard, hitting all the right notes, none of which, of course, he could see. He is one of the happiest men I have ever met.

Lord's, 23 June 1990

BRIAN JOHNSTON   Are you a jazz pianist, classical pianist or just a pianist?
GEORGE SHEARING   I'm a pianist who happens to play jazz. I have said this
quite frequently. I am also a pianist who happens to be blind, as opposed to
a blind pianist. I may get blind when my work is done, but not before.
BRIAN   We heard of your enthusiasm for cricket from, I think, a lady down
in Stow-on-the-Wold, where you come every summer. You live in America
now.
GEORGE   Yes, we've lived in New York for almost twelve years and
we lived in California before then. What do you think about the reten-
tion of my accent? Is there much?
BRIAN   There's a little tingle of American, but mostly it's the good old
basic English. And it is pretty basic – it's Battersea, isn't it?
GEORGE   It is. Until I was sixteen I was very much a Cockney and I think
the thing that got me out of being a Cockney was when I was doing
some broadcasts for the BBC and the announcer came on and said (very
properly), 'For the next fifteen minutes you will be hearing the music
of George Shearing.' I played the first medley and said, 'Good mornin'
everybody. We just played the medley of commercial popular numbers
includin' "Tears on my Pillow", "Let Me Whisper I Love You", "Magyar
Melody" and "Jeepers Creepers".' And the announcer came back after
the show to say, 'For the last fifteen minutes you have been hearing the
music of George Shearing.' Fortunately I had some good ears and I was
able to dispense with the largest part of my Cockney accent.

I was in a residential school between the ages of twelve and sixteen
– and I'm going to be 71 this August. In this school we played cricket.
Now you can imagine blind people playing cricket. First of all we played
in the gymnasium. We played with a rather large balloon-type ball with a
bell in it and all the bowling was underhand, of course, and this ball would
bounce along the gymnasium floor. The wicket was two large blocks of
wood, perhaps fifteen or sixteen inches long, bolted together with a heavy
nut and bolt on each end. Sandwiched in between was a piece of plywood,
so that we could hear this ball when it hit the wicket. You'd know very
well you were out if that happened.

BRIAN   No disputing with the umpire.

GEORGE   Dickie Bird would have no problems.

   Now, if you hit the side wall it was one run; if you hit the end wall of the gymnasium it was two runs; if you hit the end wall without a bounce it was four; if you hit the ceiling at the other end it was six and if you hit the overmantel it was three weeks' suspension.

BRIAN   Much the same rules for indoor cricket today. But – born blind – how do you picture a cricket ball or a cricket bat?

GEORGE   When I was a kid I used to go out in the street and play cricket with sighted people. And my little nephew would hold the bat with me and he would indicate when he was going to swing it. We actually did make many contacts with the bat on the ball – a regular cricket bat and ball.

BRIAN   What was your father? Was he a musician?

GEORGE   No, Daddy was a coalman. He would deliver coal.

BRIAN   With a horse and cart?

GEORGE   Yes. I often wondered if he shouldn't put on his cart: 'COAL A LA CART OR CUL DE SACK'.

BRIAN   Not a bad gag. Now, did he start you on music? How did you get into that?

GEORGE   I'm the youngest of a family of nine. There were no musicians in the family at all, so I imagine that in a previous life I was Mozart's guide dog. I don't really know how it started.

BRIAN   Can we have a look at your fingers? I'm always interested in the fingers of guitarists and pianists. Yours are fairly delicate. They're straight. They haven't been broken by a cricket ball. So when did you feel the first touch of a piano and decide that was what you wanted to do?

GEORGE   Before actually trying to make music as a pianist, I would shy bottles out of the second-storey window and hear them hit the street and they would have quite musical sounds. I had quite good taste, because I would use milk bottles for classical music and beer bottles for jazz.

BRIAN   I wouldn't talk too loud, because the police have probably got all the records. They've been looking for the chap who did that.

GEORGE   I first put my hands on a piano, I think, when I was three years of age. I was listening to the old crystal set. It was stuff like the Roy Fox band. Then I would go over to the piano and pick out the tune that I had just heard.

BRIAN   Is there such a thing as Braille music?

GEORGE   Very much so. In fact I've learnt a number of concertos in Braille and played them with many symphony orchestras in the United States. I have given that up because I'm a little afraid of memory lapse. I had one thirty-bar memory lapse, I remember, when I was playing with the Buffalo Symphony and my wife noticed that I was leaning towards the orchestra. Being, of course, a musician who plays jazz, on hearing the chords of the orchestra, I could immediately improvise in the style of Mozart until my mind decided to behave once again and go back to the score.

BRIAN   So you can do it from Braille, but basically you're an ear pianist.

GEORGE   Yes, very much. You see, if you were to do anything short of sitting on the piano, I could probably hear what you were playing. If you played a ten-note chord, I could probably hear.

BRIAN   If I sat on it it would probably be a twenty-note chord.

GEORGE   Well, I didn't say that.

BRIAN   George, do you remember when we first met?

GEORGE   Yes, it was in Fisher's Restaurant in about 1946, when we were with the Frank Weir band.

BRIAN   We did a *Saturday Night Out* when I first joined the BBC. I joined in January and this must have been about April 1946. And I was amazed then as I talked to you and I asked how you were getting home. You said, 'Oh, I've come by tube, I shall be going home by tube.'

GEORGE   And I used to do it without the aid of a cane or a dog or anything else. We've had a man in the United States who used to do that. His name was Doctor Spanner and you could prove that he did it, because he had all kinds of bruises all over his body where he'd got into various accidents. They used to refer to him as 'the Scar-Spangled Spanner'.

BRIAN   But did you tap your way along Bond Street to the tube station?

GEORGE   When I started to use a cane I did. One time during World War Two I remember somebody said to me, 'Would you see me across the road?' And I took his arm and saw him across the road. It's the only case I've heard of the blind leading the blind.

BRIAN   Do you still walk around on your own if you know the district?

GEORGE   Not very much. One tends to lose one's nerve a little bit when you pass 65, I think.

BRIAN   Oh, get away! Describe for me what you think you're looking out at here.

GEORGE   Well, we are probably at one end of the cricket field and are we looking down the length of the pitch?

BRIAN   Yes.

GEORGE   I have light and dark, but that's all I have. Sitting in this box, of course, it's an interesting aspect of controlled acoustics and wonderful daylight and fresh air coming in through open windows. As a matter of fact I wouldn't mind buying a lifetime ticket here.

BRIAN   Well, you'd be most welcome. When we say that the umpire's wearing a white coat or the batsman plays a stroke, can you figure what that means?

GEORGE   No. Two things that a born-blind man would have difficulty with are colour and perspective. When you think about it, you can be satisfied that you're looking at a table on a flat piece of paper, although it obviously has cubic capacity. And I suppose my education and my instruction gives me the information that perhaps you draw two legs shorter than the other two and something about the way the light gets it. I have no conception at all of colours. In fact, once when I got a cab in the mid-town area of Chicago, I was to meet the Count Basie band on the South Side. They were all staying at a hotel mostly frequented by black people at that time and I said to the cab driver, 'Could you take me to the South Central Hotel?' And he said, 'Do you know that's a coloured hotel?' I said, 'Really? What colour is it?' And when we got there I gave him a tip about twice the size one would normally do, to make up for his ignorance, got into the bus with the Basie band and took off and hoped that he was duly embarrassed.

BRIAN   Does green grass mean anything to you?

GEORGE   Oh, yes. What a lovely smell when it's freshly mowed and when it's been watered. It means a great deal to me. But I suppose if you want colour description, I would say that blue would be something peaceful, red would be something perhaps angry and green – I don't know.

BRIAN   Well, it's something very pleasant to look at, if you have a nice green cricket field.

You've lived in America a long time – have you always liked cricket?

GEORGE   I've always been very fond of cricket, but, as you can imagine, being in America, one has had a great many years *in absentia*, which always makes me sad and I can't wait to get over here and render my wife a cricket widow.

BRIAN   How much do you come over now?

GEORGE   Three months a year and my aim is to make it six months a year.

BRIAN   You go to the Cotswolds and do you sit and listen to the Test matches?

GEORGE   Oh, yes, of course I do. As a matter of fact, we may catch the three-thirty this afternoon, so that by five I can be in my deckchair in the garden listening to the rest of the afternoon's play. And incidentally, I think you're a very logical and wonderful follow-on from Howard Marshall.

BRIAN   Did you hear him?

GEORGE   Oh, many times.

BRIAN   Did you hear him describe Len Hutton's famous innings at the Oval – the 364?

GEORGE   Yes. I used to listen to him on the first radios I had in the thirties.

BRIAN   He was lovely to listen to. He could take his place here and show us up. In other sports, commentators of that vintage would be old-fashioned, but he would be absolutely perfect.

Are you a good impersonator? Can you pick up people's voices?

GEORGE   I used to do Norman Long monologues on my show.

BRIAN   'A song, a smile and a piano' – Norman Long.

GEORGE   (*in character*)

> I've saved up all the year for this
> And here it is, no kid.
> This here Irish Sweepstake ticket
> And it cost me half a quid
> Not much of it to look at,
> Bit expensive like, of course,
> But if I draws a winner,
> Gor, lumme, if I even draws a horse,
> The quids, just think about them,
> Thousands of them, lovely notes

Not greasy – nice and new.
I'll take me wife and family
Down to Margate by the sea.
Cockles, rock and winkles,
Shrimps and strawberries for tea.
A-sitting in your deckchairs,
With your conscience clear and sound,
A-smiling at the bloke and saying,
'Can you change a pound?'
Instead of hopping out of them
Each time the bloke comes round.
Thirty thousand quid!

BRIAN   That's marvellous. Did you get all that from memory, or did you used to write it down?

GEORGE   No, I never wrote it down. I listened to it enough until I remembered it and I've never forgotten it since 1935 or '36 when I first heard it, any more than I've forgotten the geographical version of the Lord's prayer.

BRIAN   Which is what?

GEORGE

How far is the White Hart from Hendon?
Harrow Road be thy name.
Thy Kingston come, Thy Wimbledon
In Erith as it is in Devon.
Give us this Bray our Maidenhead
And forgive us our Westminsters,
As we forgive those who Westminster against us.
And lead us not into Thames Ditton,
But deliver us from Yeovil [or from the Oval if you prefer]
For Thine is the Kingston and the Purley and the Crawley
For Iver and Iver,
Crouch End.

BRIAN   Have you ever done stand-up comedy?

GEORGE   I'm far too lazy to do stand-up comedy. I sit down at the piano because I have embraced the philosophy for lo (!) these many years, 'Why should any man work when he has the health and strength to lie in bed?'

BRIAN   You sit down at the piano. You had a quintet for many years which was famous. Did you enjoy playing with people, or do you prefer to be solo?

GEORGE   Well, I enjoyed it for 29 years. I've now pared down to just bass and piano, because I can address myself to being a more complete pianist with a much greater degree of freedom every night to create what comes into mind – obviously restricted by the chords of the particular tune that I happen to be playing.

BRIAN   Now, in addition to playing, you are a composer. How many hits have you composed?

GEORGE   Oh, I can play you a medley of my hit in two minutes. It's called 'Lullaby of Birdland'. I've composed about 99 other compositions which have gone from relative obscurity to total oblivion.

BRIAN   But what do people want? When they see you they say, 'Come on, George, play . . .' What?

GEORGE   They still want 'September in the Rain', which was one of the quintet's most famous numbers. We did 90,000 copies of that. It was a 78 when it started.

BRIAN   Now, 'Lullaby of Birdland'– I always thought that was a lovely lullaby of a little wood with the birds twittering, but Birdland wasn't actually that, was it?

GEORGE   Birdland actually was a club in New York dedicated to Charlie Parker, who was nicknamed 'the Bird' and I've played Birdland many times. It was a little basement kind of dive.

BRIAN   We have thousands of blind listeners. Any word for them about cricket and what it's meant to you?

GEORGE   I hope they enjoy cricket as much as I do, because I really love it. Incidentally, the Royal National Institute for the Blind put out the cricket fixtures in Braille.

BRIAN   If I was to ask you to sing or hum your favourite tune to finish, what would it be?

GEORGE   It would be almost anything of Cole Porter or Jerome Kern. One thing that comes to mind is:

Whenever skies look grey to me
And trouble begins to brew;
Whenever the winter wind becomes too strong,
I concentrate on you – Graham Gooch
I concentrate on you – Richard Hadlee.

Graham Taylor

Brian Johnston was ready to try his hand at most things but he always said that there were two jobs he definitely would not want to do – cricket selector and manager of the England football team. Both of them, he felt, had too much pressure and undue criticism – with the football manager having the worst of it.

Graham Taylor knew exactly what he meant when he was hounded out of his job after England's failure to qualify for the 1994 World Cup finals but he had been delighted to subject himself to Johnners' form of interrogation during a Test match at Edgbaston.

There are many reasons why people take part in media interviews. If the truth be known, most of them are egotistical – and that on occasions can be as much from the interviewer's point of view as that of the interviewee.

However, amongst the myriads which abound there are some 'jewels' where no-one is trying to score points, no-one is trying to heckle and there is a mutual respect not only for each other but also for the reader, listener or viewer.

It is difficult to describe a 'View from the Boundary' with Brian Johnston as an interview. More like popping in for a cosy chat and then afterwards realizing how many different topics have been discussed and how many times he gently and perceptively led you into revealing more about yourself and any values and beliefs you hold.

He was a man who showed a genuine interest in you, saw no reason to hurt and wanted you to do nothing else but enjoy yourself.

My visit to Edgbaston in 1991 followed the end of my first season as the England football manager. With an undefeated record in twelve games and well on the way to qualifying for the 1992 European Championships, I was however already coming under fire from the critics and it was indeed a welcome relief to be in a sporting environment where my 'inquisitor' was a man who obviously took his job far more seriously than he did himself.

This is a hard balance to achieve but Brian's irrepressible sense of humour coupled with his obvious love of cricket shed him of all pomposity and made it a pleasure to be in his company.

An honourable man with a perpetual twinkle in his eye is my lasting view of the man on the boundary.

9

DOWN YOUR WAY

Anthony Smith

———————

Brian presented Down Your Way *for fifteen years, taking over from Franklin Engelmann in 1972 and presenting exactly the same number of programmes as his predecessor – 733. Anthony Smith was his producer.*

Our next appointment was with a jeweller and we were, unusually, late. Apologies would be made and excuses offered, but he would never know the real reason for our delay. An hour and a half earlier the *Down Your Way* team had been marooned in the middle of a West Country river. A red-faced Harbourmaster, in official uniform, had made us promise that we would not reveal that a trip in his launch, flag proudly flying, had ended, certainly in embarrassment, and almost in disaster.

We had thought it would be a nice idea to back our interview with him with actuality. We would talk to him, we thought, on board his launch at the river's estuary. The trip down stream had been pleasant and uneventful but our timetable was a tight one and we were always going to be against the clock. The river was tidal and the tide when it went out did so very rapidly, leaving behind thick deep mud. Our helmsman for no explicable reason steered to port when he should have gone to starboard and we became stuck fast at least thirty feet from the riverbank.

Brian Johnston took it all with his usual good humour. There was always in every situation a funny side for him. At first there was a dispute as to whether I as the producer and, as I saw it, the captain of the *Down Your Way* team or the Harbourmaster should be the last to leave the boat. We were not in any danger, of course, but *Down Your Way* recordings were like holiday outings and good-natured banter was always very much the code.

The boat would not refloat, naturally, for at least twelve hours and to remain on board was out of the question. Off came Brian's shoes and socks, and with trousers rolled up to his knees he slipped over the side of the boat and down into the mud. By the time he had waded to the bank he was covered in the stuff. His next problem was how to get cleaned up.

He had landed in the Municipal Park. It was holiday time and the park was full of people enjoying the sunshine. There was nowhere to hide. With shoes and socks held aloft, smiling as always and giving the impression that there was nothing at all unusual in what he was doing, Brian strode into the ladies changing room of some nearby tennis courts – there was not a Gents in sight – only to find that the only water to be had was in the WC.

I can see him now. First one leg and then the other went down the pan and with the Harbourmaster pulling the chain repeatedly the mud was gradually removed. There was to be no such indignity for the producer: he had been piggy-backed ashore by the Harbourmaster.

If Brian ever told this story he would not have revealed its location. He had said he would not, to spare the Harbourmaster's blushes, and his sense of honour was such that he would never go back on his word. For me this was just one incident in our long association. It is by no means the most important or significant but just something that sprang to mind as I began to write this and to recall a man whose company it was always a pleasure to be in.

Over a period of twelve years I travelled thousands of miles with Johnners. There is not a corner of Britain that we did not visit. Once, just once, we took *Down Your Way* across the world to Australia. Heaven knows what they made of our rather old-fashioned BBC Radio programme in Alice Springs. There in the very centre of Australia, Johnners, who loved that country, went through the *Down Your Way* routine just as he would have done in Middle Wallop or Inverbervie.

I do not think that either of us were aware as we stood talking to the Warden outside the Old Telegraph Station on a scorchingly hot day in Alice that we were standing on yet another riverbank. We were on a bank of the River Todd but there was not the tiniest drop of water to be seen. Earlier in the day we had visited a camel farm and Brian, as always obliging to the photographers or in this case the photographer, as Alice Springs only boasted one, had ridden a camel round the paddock for all the world like an Indian maharajah. He was enjoying himself thoroughly.

In light-hearted mood he launched into his interview beside the 'river'. Extolling the virtues of life in Alice Springs the Warden suddenly remarked that we should really have come on Boat Race day. Without a river in sight, however puzzled Brian may have been he gave no sign, but I could see the laughter in his eyes and realized that an onset of the famous giggles was not far away. They started moments later when, warming to his theme, the Warden explained that although the River Todd was dry for most of the year this didn't deter the town of Alice Springs from having an annual Boat Race. It was staged at the height of summer. They simply cut the bottoms out of their boats and ran with them. Their Boat Race was as good as any staged on the Thames! Brian's acute sense of the ridiculous overcame him.

Brian's friendliness endeared him to people. He loved to tease and would do so repeatedly to engage and relax his interviewees. A favourite trick as we toured a factory, which we seemed to do at least once a week, was to note a nameplate on a piece of machinery. Then a few moments later having moved on a few paces, he would halt our guide and say something like, 'If I'm not mistaken that machine back there is a such and such. Wasn't it made in Darlington?' The guide's enthusiasm for such a knowledgeable visitor was immediately apparent, and there would be no stopping him when the microphone was eventually produced.

For all good interviewers, and Brian was one of the best, the ability to listen and be interested is essential. Johnners was always genuinely interested. He loved the little snippets of information, perhaps useless in themselves, that we would chance upon. They gave colour and added to the story. He learned that the longest granite step in Britain is at a public building in Penzance, and from a miller in West Wales the origin of the saying, 'He'll never set the Thames on fire.' It was all wonderful material for a person who was naturally curious and had the greatest skill in getting others to show off their knowledge and the pride that they had in their corner of the world.

This was *Down Your Way* and this was a very important part of Brian's life. He loved people and undoubtedly they loved him. Our routine never varied. As the producer I would go ahead and choose the people that the next day he would interview. That evening we would meet in our hotel for dinner. After exchanging the news from London, gossip from the Test match commentary box, news of our families or whatever, the question he asked was always the same, 'What have we got tomorrow, Old Boy?'

I would give him the timetable, outline the story, and he would soon be away to his bed with a cheery, 'Goodnight.' The next morning he would be at Reception, bill paid, bags packed, eager and ready to start work. Then for six hours without stopping we would go from cottage to castle, from farm to factory, recording our interviews.

Brian would stand pad in hand jotting down the occasional one word note and then when he was ready there would come the announcement, 'Well, I'm broody.' It was the signal that he was ready to record. The recorder was switched on and the chat was under way. The final question was always the same, 'We would like you please to choose a piece of music.'

For years *Down Your Way* was broadcast every Sunday teatime with a weekday morning repeat. It was listened to by over a million people every week. Brian insisted that the programme portrayed the good things about Britain and that we were positive. It was not difficult to do because Brian's approach to life and his warmth and personality evoked this kind of response.

It was a sad day for me when we arrived at his beloved Lord's to record Brian's last show. He had done 732 programmes and he was only going to do one more because he did not think it somehow quite right to do more programmes than his predecessor Franklin Engelmann. The photographers were out in force and someone had

had the bright idea of fixing the scoreboard to read '733 Not Out'. It was a lovely if somewhat sad day.

We lunched at Lord's and Brian gave me a silver tankard inscribed in his own inimitable handwriting. He thanked me 'for so many happy days of fun and friendship.'

With so many memories the pleasure was all mine.

10

THE BOAT RACE

From 1947 until 1989, Brian commentated on the Boat Race even though he was very much a dry bob and always had been.

It may have had something to do with the fact that his boss discovered that Brian's father had been an Oxford blue, rowing in the 1899 and 1900 Boat Races – though on each occasion the Dark Blues lost!

Nevertheless he was just as much at home on the water as he was everywhere else as Dan Topolski, the celebrated Oxford coach, discovered.

Daniel Topolski

'Welcome aboard, Toppers,' was B.J.'s cheery greeting on my first trip out on the BBC Boat Race launch. His deft, easy way of including you immediately within the tight coterie of 'friends of Brian' and fellow broadcasters made you feel at home straight away and helped dispel first-night nerves.

Johnners was generous like that and he made the whole terrifying business of live commentating seem like the best possible fun. Even the gaffes were a hoot – all part of the Johnners magic. And it made commentating on the Boat Race with him, for the last two of his forty-two years and my first two, pure pleasure.

He was a consummate professional, but of the old school. None of the 'search and destroy' interviewing techniques that are *de rigueur* today. Johnners wanted you to remember the experience of being interviewed by him with enjoyment rather than dismay. And when the boot was on the other foot when, for instance, I interviewed him a couple of years ago as a guest presenter of *Down Your Way* down on the hard next to Chiswick Bridge, he gently chided the new programme format's lack of musical interludes with a full-throated version of the 'Eton Boating Song'. There, for a moment joined all together, was a choice selection of some of the defining episodes of his life – Eton, *Down Your Way*, the Boat Race, his New College, Oxford, background and joyfully broadcasting to his beloved and adoring audience. Only the cricket was missing.

Whatever Brian did he always made sure he had fun doing it. On a radio quiz programme we did together I was pitted against him and came out very much the worse for wear. His humour and ease behind the mike and his total lack of concern at making mistakes were a joy to behold until you realized he was running circles around you. For his general knowledge was boundless and his expertise in playing to an audience supreme.

But he was never ungracious, always the gentleman. There were no sides to him, none of the cynicism or slickness that passes today for good broadcasting. What you saw was what you got.

His own sporting activity at Oxford was strictly of the 'dry bob' variety although he loved to relate how his father rowed for Oxford in the 1900 Boat Race when they lost by twenty lengths – the greatest margin in history. He was also possessed of that charming sportsman's weakness for retiring and then making popular comebacks. One would be forgiven, for instance, for not realizing that officially he retired from the BBC's cricket commentary team in 1972. So, of course, we did not really believe that he was serious when he announced in 1989 that he was leaving the Boat Race team to join his old sparring partners John Snagge and Tom Sutton in retirement. But sadly that time it was for real and he was sorely missed, especially when for the next two years the pursuing launch broke down before Hammersmith Bridge, no doubt in protest at his departure. Oh, how we needed his ad-libbing genius at those dire moments.

We were last in touch over the appeal for the renovation of our old New College cricket pavilion. He was the energetic appeal chairman and his association with the fund-raising events ensured that the money came flooding in. No-one could refuse Johnners.

11

THE GENTLEMAN

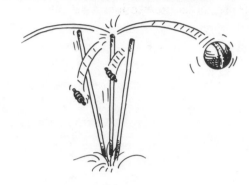

Louis Dunn

'One of the difficulties of this life is that gentlemen are fast disappearing and Mr Johnston was definitely one of them,' wrote Louis Dunn, master in charge of cricket at Keil School at Dumbarton in Scotland, when he heard of Brian's death.

'His example and good character were, at all times, one of the greatest teaching aids open to me in all the coaching I have done.'

Brian Johnston was a gentleman above all else. And he was a southern English gentleman, an example of the breed at its best. Perhaps it was this that added most to the fun of *Test Match Special*, the wonderful contrast between the professional Yorkshire bulldog of Trueman, and Johnners' delightful, light manner. I will remember him in many ways. First, of course, must come cricket. There was something about him which typified all that is best about the game. Cricket is about winning, yes, but that is not all. It isn't even most of it. The main thing is taking part, and taking part with as much style as you can possibly muster.

Brian's commentaries revealed a man who had no time for the 'win at all costs' mentality which is so prevalent nowadays. Ball tampering and sharp practice had no place as far as he was concerned. As a coach, I have to struggle against the frankly poor example which many of our most famous cricketers give. How can you tell a fielder to get the ball in as quickly as possible, no matter where it is on the pitch, when he can see Philip DeFreitas casually toss the ball further out from square leg, so allowing, through his sheer dilatoriness, the Australians an extra run? Others would tell you that that is all part of the game, that it's all right because they would have got the run anyway. But you never know. 'On ne sait jamais,' to quote P. H. Edmonds. The best coaching aid, in terms of simple cricket behaviour, that I have is a half-hour tape comprising Brian's comments about play and about how things should be done.

This is not to say that he couldn't comment on the play. Far from it – there was a fine eye, tutored not only at Eton, but also over many, many years of watching and playing which, through its experience and his own intellect, could give, in a few words, a portrait of the entire field of play. This is where radio wins over television – a skilled commentator can describe in a few seconds what a camera cannot cover in thirty. He was always ready to praise, and praise well, what he saw as good play, but never slow to comment where he didn't like what he saw. Brian Johnston epitomized for me what cricket is about. He enjoyed the game. He enjoyed the company, the chat on the side as you wait to go in, or sit having come off. Can you think of anything more pleasant than being greeted by Brian after a golden duck? There would be chaffing and jokes, but bags of support and, before you knew it, there would be a stiff gin and all would be forgotten.

He didn't have Arlott's graceful, rolling sentences, but then, is fine prose best suited to describing a game of cricket where situations can change so quickly? No, fine prose is best used when the reader or listener has time to enjoy it, when the time spent honing can be put into the reading. The commentary box is no place for that. The commentary box serves to house *commentators* who comment on the action as it happens and survey the scene, and this is where Brian was at his best, summing up not only the play, but also the atmosphere. Somewhere, I have a tape of his Coronation commentary, and the same skill is evident there, just as it was in *Down Your Way* and *In Town Tonight*.

He would laugh and joke along, and then come out with a wicked summation of play. I suspect that Brian had a deal with God – he'd stock up on stories and then ask the Almighty for rain so that he and Fred Trueman and Henry Blofeld and all the rest could just sit back and regale us. He was the man in the pavilion, the fellow who was never at a loss for a joke, and who enjoyed hearing other people's. Thinking about Brian Johnston as I write, all I can hear is his laugh, the laugh of an eighty-year-old schoolboy who still found life as much fun as when he was born. That's the point, really, that I want to bring out – Brian was always keen and enthusiastic for each new venture.

But cricket was not all. I remember Sunday afternoons would follow a routine in our house of Benny Green, Alan Dell, *Sing Something Simple* and then *Down Your Way*. Brian chatting to people he met as he travelled to one town or another around Britain. Again, there would be evident this overwhelming joy and glorious interest in what was said to him. Which brings us back to Brian Johnston the gentleman. Too few people in this life actually listen to what is said to them and are far too keen to get in their own contribution. Listen to any edition of *Down Your Way* and you'll learn all you need to know about how to get on with people.

None of what Brian did was easy. Many years ago I offered to commentate on a school sports. I ended up monosyllabic for fear of tripping up. Commentating is damn hard work and he was damn good at it. I wanted his job. Still do. But I could never do it, never handle all those facts and keep up the flow of chat at the same time and then, to cap it all, make it look so *easy*. Getting a man you've never met before to talk for a minute and a half about his town and then, at the end of that, to have him tell you exactly what the listener wanted to know – now that's art.

I never met Brian Johnston. My grandfather did many years ago when Brian was presenting something or other to someone or other. All my comments have to be viewed through that. His persona was that of the pleasant chap in the Members' Enclosure, the bloke at the Surrey end. But there was much more to him than that.

Jocelyn Galsworthy

Brian Johnston's personality appealed to all sorts of people and to both sexes. Indeed he must have done more than anyone to 'sell' cricket to the ladies. The artist, Jocelyn Galsworthy, who, in recent times, has made a speciality out of painting cricket grounds, is but one example of many.

I first met Brian Johnston in the early sixties on the Purbeck Isle in Dorset. My family had a holiday cottage at Worth Matravers and Brian and Pauline had a cottage in the nearby stone quarry village of Acton. It was undeveloped and wonderfully wild. We were introduced by my father's stockbroker whose brother-in-law was MP for Poole and had a house across the ferry at Sandbanks. I was in my early twenties and embarking on my career as a professional artist and Brian, at my request, sat for a line drawing as a favour. This was a typically kind gesture, as was the commission to paint their lovely cottage. Even in those days cricket was my great love so Brian was very much a hero to my brother and myself.

In 1988 the Johnstons came to my Exhibition at Sunningdale School where their grandsons are now pupils. They certainly took an interest in my career and from what I heard approved of the progress! In 1992, while painting Paul Getty's XI v. I Zingari at Wormsley, Brian and Pauline were obviously agreeably surprised and delighted that I was depicting that lovely new ground in all its glory.

Last year, 1993, I was back there again, this time nearer the marquee! Brian never failed to come and chatter, usually bringing with him someone special from the cricket world whom he knew I would love to meet. He would always leave them with me – Ray Lindwall, Bill Frindall, etc., etc. The painting did not advance very quickly but Brian's thought and kindness were outstanding, matched only by Pauline's and their family's encouragement and obvious joy at my love of painting cricket.

In September I wrote to Brian asking him to sit for a portrait to be included in my Exhibition in London next May – the reply was 'Contact me in January and I will know my dates!' He explained the autumn was full of his *Evening with Johnners* and charity 'dos' which brings me sadly to my last memory of him. On 12 November 1993 at a Cricket Society dinner at Lord's Hubert Doggart said to me, 'Are you not going to see Johnners at the Windsor Theatre?' As I have a studio near Windsor I felt very bad at having missed the notices for the show and contacted the theatre at once to no avail – it was completely sold out. I telephoned again the next day, Sunday 14 November. They had one return in the stalls. It was the most wonderful experience to have Brian to 'oneself' as it were for two hours. The audience of all ages was enthralled – it was one long amazing laugh. I was so thankful to have experienced such a unique performance and to have such a vivid lasting memory. He was beyond compare.

Rachael Heyhoe-Flint

If the ladies liked Brian, then Brian certainly liked the ladies – as Rachael Heyhoe-Flint, former captain of the England women's team, explains.

I have always looked upon Johnners as a great friend and genuine supporter of women's cricket – so much so that when I co-authored *Fair Play*, the History of Women's Cricket (Heyhoe-Flint and Rheiberg, Angus & Robinson, 1976), I asked Brian to write the foreword to the book. His foreword gives such a good impression of what he thought of our game – and I now unashamedly reproduce an extract from it.

> I am seldom so presumptuous as to disagree with an opinion expressed by a revered England cricket captain – but I did do so once. The ex-captain was Len Hutton and the occasion was a match on Chislehurst Green between Colin Cowdrey's XI and the England Women's XI. I was keeping wicket and Len was standing at slip. I asked him what he thought of women playing cricket. He gave me a funny look and answered: 'It's just like a man trying to knit, isn't it?'

But as I've said I disagreed – and incidentally the women won the match!

In fact I have always supported the girls and think that they've got quite a lot to teach us men. First-class cricket tends nowadays to be rather dull and scientific or 'professional' as it's so often called. The ladies bring a touch of grace to what is essentially a graceful game. Anyone who has watched women play recently will know that as bats*men* they *use* their feet to the slow bowlers; have all the strokes and run like hinds between the wickets. In the old days if you wished to insult a fielder you told him that he threw like a girl. Nowadays their returns from the outfield come whistling back over the top of the stumps. Their fielding is remarkably keen and their bowling subtle and steady. The one thing they lack is pace and I am sure they make up for that off the field!

I have played quite a bit of cricket with women. At my private school the headmaster's daughter, Kitten, bowled a nifty leg-break and in the holidays we used to play a mixed match in the village of Much Marcle in Herefordshire. The star was a retired bishop's wife called Mrs Whitehead. She was a left-hander and defended dourly and usually carried her bat. In later years I saw her exact replica in test cricket – Slasher Mackay, the impassive Australian – though Mrs Whitehead did not chew gum!

Mothers too have played an important part in cricket. Perhaps the best example is in Australia where Vic Richardson's daughter, Mrs Chappell, coached her three sons, Ian, Greg and Trevor, in the back garden with results we in England know all to well. Penny Cowdrey too is another mother brought up on garden cricket where her bowling has for years tested her three sons – Christopher, Jeremy and Graham. Her greatest triumph came last summer when she took 5 wickets against Graham's Junior School XI and they say that her swingers that day were practically unplayable!

Even more important to me personally was the fact that early on in our courtship I discovered that my wife Pauline could throw a cricket ball really well, as befitted a Yorkshire girl. I won't pretend that it was a vital factor in our romance but it helped!

I hope by now that it is obvious that I am 100 per cent behind women's cricket but there is one small change which I would
like to see. I wish they would wear trousers instead of those
divided skirts. I'm always worried that the pad straps will chafe
at the back of their knees! I would also like to see them get
more coverage on radio and television though I can see one or
two pitfalls for commentators: what girl would enjoy hearing that
she has got two short legs – one of them square! On the other
hand she would not, I'm sure, complain if she heard that she had a
very fine leg!

I first met Johnners at that match he referred to in his foreword, at
Chislehurst – it was in 1963; while I was batting I realized that perhaps
what his wicket-keeping lacked in international skill, his ability at chatting
up was worth a wicket or two! Jim Laker was bowling and Johnners bet
me a fiver that I couldn't hit Jim back over the sightscreen for six.
Ever one for a challenge, I took the bait, lashed out, and was caught
by Peter Walker, high above his head just in front of the sightscreen.
Damn it – Johnston 1 Heyhoe 0.

My whole family loved Johnners – husband Derrick was always 'Flinters',
youngest son Ben was 'Benners' and I was 'Heyhers'. Dear Johnners
always invited me into the *Test Match Special* commentary box and
gave me the honourable mention; the supply of cakes was endless and
I so loved Brian's expressions of delight as each offering was delivered; I think the cake which must have given him most moments of
mirth was delivered to the Edgbaston commentary box during a Test
there in 1992 – a vast couple of pink mounds depicting a lady's fulsome
bust with two glacé cherries strategically placed; the mirth in the box
was unconfined with Johnners leading the not too stifled giggles and
hilarious schoolboy-like actions as he and his fellow commentators decided how to devour the offering!

I've worked with Johnners on Radio 4's *Test Match Trivia*, and the
fun he managed to generate, with his double entendres and quick wit,
turned the programme into a very popular series; he had such amazing
quickness of thought and wit for someone still broadcasting in his eighties

– and he was always a very warm and generous host to me as one of the few women on the panel.

When I wanted to see if I could become the first woman to join the MCC, I instantly thought of Johnners as one of my sponsors – together with Tim Rice, Dennis Amiss and Sir Jack Hayward. Johnners' support was unwavering, both as a sponsor on my application form – and then as proposer of the motion for the 1990 AGM 'that women should be allowed to apply for membership of the MCC'.

Even though the motion was defeated by a vast margin Johnners was still willing to support the campaign in subsequent years. In December 1992 when I had sought his advice as to when to try again, he wrote to me, 'I still think it *should* happen but I do not think the time is right. The members gave their verdict two years ago and I think it would be annoying to them and I fear unproductive. Sorry if I appear uncooperative but I think what I think is *wise*. You are a great girl and I *like* you! Yours ever Johnners.'

And I too liked Johnners for his wise counsel and very much respected advice.

I remember when I first applied for membership and Johnners was interviewed on TV as to why he supported my efforts. He replied that he felt it was time the MCC did change their attitudes, but that he felt bold enough to support me because he bet that women would never become members in his lifetime. Sadly that prediction was accurate – but how I wished Johnners could have been immortal, because I was so looking forward to inviting him to the celebration party.

RIP Johnners – the Flintstones all love and miss you.

12

A FAMILY MAN

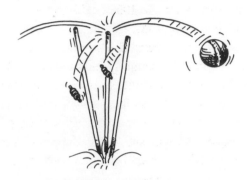

Pauline Johnston

A Day in the Life of Brian Johnston

How do you condense forty-five years into 500 words? A typical day in
our lives might be a good start.

7.30–7.45 a.m., wake up, listen to *Today* on Radio 4 till eight o'clock.
Sometimes Brian would be asked to make comments on an event to do
with cricket, so he would do a live broadcast on the telephone straight into
the *Today* programme. This actually happened on the morning of his heart
attack. The telephone woke us up with a start at 7.15 a.m. and he was
asked to comment on the name change of the Famous Bat & Ball Inn at
Hambledon – so he spoke about it on air – whilst having his breakfast! After
that he complained of indigestion, which he never suffered from, so I gave
him an indigestion tablet to suck. This was actually a sign of an impending
heart attack, but I didn't know that at the time. If only I had . . .

Anyway, usually after breakfast he shaved and went into his study to
cope with his large pile of mail, eight to ten letters a day – still in his
pyjamas. He'd stay there, answering each one by hand on his pale blue

postcards to his many admirers. Sometimes he would send a saucy seaside postcard to an old friend and shock their wives and the postman! If he had a lunch engagement he would stay in his dressing gown until it was time to bathe, and then dress in the suit he wanted to wear rather than change twice.

He often padded down to open the front door in his pyjamas (as he would say, what a funny place to keep a door!) and couldn't care less who saw him! When he was at home, we would have a proper lunch, cooked by Cally, Mrs Callander, our wonderful housekeeper, who has been with us for thirty-three and a half years. She has been the backbone of our family life of five children, and helped me to look after them all – and Brian! He loved to pull her leg, which she always took in her stride. Her daughter, Ann, typed the manuscripts of Brian's many books and somehow managed to decipher his rather bad handwriting! Then we would watch *Neighbours* together. Very often the phone would ring immediately it finished and Paul Getty and Brian would have a good giggle and chat about it like two schoolboys!

He loved doing the *Daily Telegraph* crossword every day and would sit with it on his knee till late in the evening, trying to finish it, with a little help from me, but I wasn't very good at it. After *Neighbours* he had a short 'kip' for twenty to thirty minutes, which revitalized him, and I often did the same; it was a cosy thing to do and I miss that now.

Every day Brian would find time to go for a short walk, whether it was fine or dull. He would post his letters and continue 'round the block' as a form of exercise, because he had often been sitting writing his book, or writing pieces for other people's books or articles after completing his letters, and felt the need to stretch out. He always said he paced himself, but I'm afraid his talks and travels overtook these good intentions to a great degree.

In the summer he would clip the edges of the lawn and dig out weeds from the paths – but he was forbidden to touch the flowerbeds as he didn't know a weed from a plant! I gave him an arbour for his eightieth birthday and he christened it 'Sydney' – so we'd go there at teatime when the sun reached the end of the garden and sit in Sydney. After tea he would return to his study and write again – he never wanted a secretary for his fan mail as he preferred to answer each one individually – he coped with all his own VAT returns and other business correspondence as well as making arrangements for speeches and dinners and BBC work. It was never ending and quite a heavy burden on him. If we went away on holiday it took weeks for him to catch up on his back correspondence on top of the everyday pile that seemed to increase all the time. He would never turn down a request for help and would say, 'How can I refuse, what *can* I do?' when someone asked him to do something in a year's time!

In the last six months he had decided not to do any more after-dinner speeches and to concentrate solely on his stage show *An Evening with Johnners*. He really loved having the audiences laughing at his jokes and in spite of my protestation had booked several more to do this year. 'Don't stop me doing something I really enjoy,' he would say. A car would come and collect him in the afternoon and he would creep in at about midnight trying not to wake me up, but it was difficult to relax until I knew he was safely home.

Between 7 and 8 p.m. he would frequently ring up his old friends and kept in touch with the ever-increasing number of their widows. They loved to hear from him and really appreciated his concern for them.

Our normal bedtime was eleven o'clock and a short read in bed first. He loved a cup of Ovaltine to help him sleep – memories of childhood I suppose, 'We are the Ovaltinies, happy boys and girls,' which 'Uncle' Mac used to sing on the radio when I was a child! Those were the days, now gone for ever with the passing of his generation.

Lynda Lee-Potter

———

Above everything else, Brian Johnston was a family man, utterly devoted to his wife, Pauline, and their five children. Lynda Lee-Potter of the Daily Mail *visited Pauline at their St John's Wood home not long after Brian died.*

The indented cushion is still on Brian Johnston's chair in his study. The notes for his new book are on his desk, his wristwatch and loose change are in the ash tray.

The room is crammed with the memorabilia of a lifetime – pictures, awards, trophies, endless reference books on cricket. Any moment, one expects the celebrated broadcaster to walk into the room.

'I'm so used to him being away, I still keep thinking he's coming back,' says his beloved wife, Pauline. 'He never came into the house without giving his little whistle.'

When the star of *Test Match Special* had his heart attack in a taxi at the beginning of December, it was reported in every newspaper. When he died a month later, the eulogies by friends and colleagues were unprecedented in their admiration and love.

Like all families, the Johnstons had their sad times. Their youngest daughter Joanna, 28, was born with Down's Syndrome and was later diagnosed a diabetic. But mostly their house was, and is, full of laughter. Pauline's memories of her husband are joyful and there are no if-onlys or regrets.

'I've had such a wonderful marriage for forty-five years to a wonderful man. We had five children, seven grandchildren, I feel fulfilled,' she says. 'Why should I crack up? Brian wouldn't want me to do that, it wasn't his way.

'People say "Oh, you'll have good days and bad days, you'll get fits of depression", but I haven't had them yet. Brian did everything he wanted to and he went out right at the top. I am sad inside, but I keep it to myself. I'm just so grateful for what we had.

'People look at me and say "You're looking better than I expected", but the one thing Brian couldn't stand was people moping about. The memorial service in Westminster Abbey will be one of celebration. I don't want anybody in black.'

Pauline Johnston is tall with blue eyes, a lovely skin and endless upper-class charm. She was born Pauline Tozer and grew up, like her husband, in an old-fashioned privileged milieu. Her great-grandfather was one of the founders of United Steel, and of the Yorkshire County Cricket Club. She met her future husband through her brother, who'd been in the Grenadier Guards with Brian during the war. When Pauline got a job at the BBC, he said, 'Brian Johnston works there, why don't you give him a ring?' She did, he invited her out to lunch, fell in love with her instantly and proposed almost immediately.

They were engaged a month after they met and married five months later in April 1948. She wanted the wedding to be in June but he said: 'Terribly sorry, can't have that, it's the cricket season.'

After his heart attack and a spell in St Mary's Hospital, Paddington, Pauline got her husband transferred to King Edward VII Hospital for Officers, near Harley Street, and then took him home. 'I had a lovely New Zealand girl called Sarah to help me. Our GP called once. At Christmas, it was just Sarah, Brian and me. It was the saddest day I'd ever had. I bought a tiny little plum pudding from Marks & Spencer, the smallest turkey I could find. It was the first time for forty-five years I hadn't had a huge family Christmas. We were normally fifteen.

'We just went from day to day, really. He could play card games, he could write, but he couldn't remember anything. On the Friday before he died I took him for a walk round Lord's, and I'm so pleased now that I did that. I parked the car and we walked arm in arm right round the ground. I pointed out the commentary box. I said, "What's that?" and he said "*Test Match Special*".

'Joanna came home and she'd always loved card games, so the three of us played together. She could read by the time she was seven.'

Her five children have been a powerful support, though there was added trauma in the fact that her son Ian was travelling around South America and they weren't able to get in touch with him for several days.

Her eldest son, Barry, came in the ambulance with her to take Brian back to hospital, while Andrew and daughter Clare were with her when he died. 'We held his hands and talked and told him we loved him and he knew we were there.'

He's buried now in Swanage, where they've had a holiday home overlooking the sea for more than thirty years.

'At the funeral we sang *All Things Bright and Beautiful,*' says Pauline. 'There were about twenty-five members of the family, our housekeeper Cally – Mrs Callander, who's been the backbone of our lives for thirty-three years – and friends from Swanage. The full choir turned out and then afterwards we went to the Mowlem theatre restaurant.

'I'd asked them if they'd put on a buffet and I specially requested little chocolate cakes which Brian loved. Afterwards, somebody sent me this marvellous cartoon showing Archangel Gabriel at the Pearly Gates saying: "Anybody expecting a chocolate cake?"

'Brian was always cheerful, never depressed, never ill. He believed in finding the goodness in people. He'd say sometimes, "No, that wouldn't be ethical." I told him he was too good to be true, but he was always right about people. He sensed whether they were good or not. If somebody upset him, behaved badly, he didn't want to speak to them again.

'We didn't actually tell each other we loved each other a lot, except on wedding anniversaries and Christmas, but we knew it.'

Just three months before he died, Brian and son Barry – a presenter for Radio Solent – appeared on Kilroy together. It was an early morning programme about fathers and sons and Brian said he didn't think he'd ever told his son he loved him. He turned to Barry and said: 'I love you.' Barry said: 'I love you, too.' They then went home to Pauline to have breakfast and she remembers them walking in, both clearly feeling very emotional.

'It was strange, because Brian wasn't a demonstrative man. Even when the boys went off to prep school, he'd just shake their hands and say: "Goodbye old man." It was the way he was brought up. He never kissed the boys, though they in recent years sometimes kissed him on top of his head. And they all absolutely adored him.

'He had a marvellous philosophy of "Do as you would be done by", which just endeared him to people. I'm a Yorkshire girl and if I'd ever been a bit abrupt to anybody, he'd say: "Why did you do that?" He was my guide, my friend, he made me laugh.

'We made a really good pair, but we were so different. I love dancing, classical music, art galleries. He loved music hall and wouldn't sit through wordy plays. I went along with the cricket, and I enjoyed going to matches. I'd sit at the back of the commentary box and the chaps are such a lovely lot. They'd say: "Have a cake, Polly."

'Brian appeared to be casual, but he was the absolute professional, so punctual. I was always ten minutes late, but he'd had a military career and he'd had to work with a stopwatch on *In Town Tonight*. When he met me it was a bit of a shock to the system.'

The Johnstons' party on the Friday of the first Test at Lord's is legendary in cricket circles. They always had a marquee in the garden and Brian had already booked their regular butler, Beau, for this year's party. 'Somebody told me the other day that Tim Rice was having a bet with somebody as to whether or not I would hold the party without Brian. Tim said he thought I would, and he's won his bet.'

Right up until he had his heart attack, Brian Johnston was working flat out. The day he was taken ill he was on his way to speak at a lunch in Bristol, the next day he had a lunch scheduled in Nottingham. He'd also had a huge success with his one-man show, *An Evening with Johnners*. 'All those two-hour one-man shows were incredibly exhausting,' says Pauline. 'But he kept saying "Don't try to stop me, I'm happy doing them", and look what happened.

'It was too much, to work as hard as that at eighty-one, but he was doing it for the grandchildren's school fees and he loved it. But he would never be paid for speaking at cricket dinners. He used to say: "I've got so much out of cricket, I want to put something back."

'We kept each other young. He'd had a bit of sciatica, but he insisted he was good at pacing himself. He always had a little snooze in the afternoon after *Neighbours*. He and Paul Getty were great *Neighbours* fans, it cemented their friendship. I bought him an arbour for his eightieth birthday which he christened "Sydney" – for obvious reasons! When we used to take tea in the garden, Brian would say: "We're going to have tea in Sydney." Daft isn't it?

'He always pulled everybody's legs, he saw double entendres in everything. He never ever grew up. My father was a colonel in the Territorial Army and when he first met Brian he said: "Is that man ever serious?" '

When Brian was still in hospital, Pauline asked the taxi driver who had driven him there with such speed if he'd call and see her. 'This very large, black driver came round and I said: "Do you know who your passenger was?" He said: "No, ma'am."

'I pointed to Brian's picture and I said: "Do you come from the West Indies?" He said: "No, ma'am, Nigeria." I said: "Do you like cricket?" He said: "I can't stand it, football's my game."

'I explained what Brian did, and I tried to give him some money, but he wouldn't take it. He's called Akim Akimode and he's such a lovely man. I kept in touch, and when Brian came home from hospital the Thursday before Christmas I asked him to come round to meet Brian and they shook hands.

'My father once came to lunch at 55 Portland Place, which was the BBC's outside broadcasting office. Brian and his friends used to play cricket in the office. If you hit the window it was a six. My father walked in and Brian said: "Hang on a minute colonel, just got to finish this over." '

Pauline recently found the baby book which Brian's mother had kept on her infant son. Written on one page was 'He laughed at a fortnight', which seems prophetic.

He was a born entertainer, a life enhancer, a joyful original. But amid all the glowing praise bestowed upon him in the letters, one phrase – 'He was a good man, and a real gentleman' – illuminates the simple truth. *(Reproduced with permission from the* Daily Mail.*)*

Barry Johnston

Barry Johnston, Brian's eldest son, followed his father into radio but was always more interested in pop music than cricket.

In 1982 I was living in Los Angeles when I received a letter from Thames Television. They were going to feature my father on *This Is Your Life* and wondered if I would like to take part in the programme. At the time

I was playing the piano in a cocktail bar to pay the rent so I could hardly believe my luck when they offered a free return air fare to London.

It was all terribly secret. When I arrived at Heathrow I rang home, but my father answered so I had to put the phone down. I discovered that all the subjects on *This Is Your Life* are given code names so that nobody finds out before the programme. For obvious reasons Brian had been nicknamed 'Mr Cake' and when I checked into the hotel I had to sign in as Barry Cake!

We all knew Brian secretly longed to be on the programme. He watched it every week and used to roar with laughter at the way Eamonn Andrews introduced the guests. He especially enjoyed the end where Eamonn would produce the surprise guest with the words 'You haven't seen her for ten years, you thought she was in New Zealand but no, we've flown her 10,000 miles to be with you tonight . . .' and so on.

The day after I arrived in London we all had to attend a script meeting with Eamonn and the production staff. Because Brian knew the programme so well he was bound to guess that they would fly me back from California and my brother Andrew from Sydney in Australia. So instead of keeping him in suspense they planned to bring us on near the beginning. But when we read the script we saw that Eamonn was going to introduce us without those famous words. We had to insist that he put in, 'You thought he was in Los Angeles but no . . . ' even though he complained it was corny and predictable – because that's exactly why Brian loved the programme.

Brian was caught completely by surprise and was absolutely thrilled to be the subject. But even so he wanted to keep up appearances. The one thing he didn't like was to be hugged and kissed in public. I'd been in America and hadn't seen him for eighteen months so it was quite an emotional reunion but as I walked up to him to give him a pat on the back he whispered, 'We don't kiss, do we?' I said, 'No, but Andrew's going to give you a big wet one!' When Andrew came out next you could see Brian looking exceedingly nervous.

I was asked if I could think of a story that would sum up Brian as a father. The only one I could think of was a perfect example of his attitude to fatherhood and to life.

Brian loved his traditional Sunday lunch with the family, especially roast beef and Yorkshire pudding or roast chicken with lots of bread sauce, and it was always prompt at one o'clock. One weekend when I was eighteen and still living at home I spent my first Saturday night at a girlfriend's flat. Being the dutiful son I turned up for Sunday lunch the next day but I was about half an hour late and looking very much the worse for wear. They'd already started without me and Mum wasn't too pleased. As I sat down Brian said he'd like a word with me afterwards and I thought I was in for a rocket, or at least a lecture on the facts of life.

After lunch I was in my bedroom when he knocked on the door. 'Let me give you some advice,' he said, 'whatever you get up to with a girlfriend on Saturday night is entirely up to you, just don't be late for lunch on Sunday – it does upset your mother!' It was excellent advice and I've remembered it ever since.

And after all that, he never did tell me the facts of life.

Andrew Johnston

Andrew Johnston, Brian's second son, who works in publishing, remembers how one of his father's jokes misfired . . .

Sitting at my father's desk, surrounded by the comforts of his life, the memories inevitably come flooding back, and it seems impossible to give adequate justice in words to a man who has been so central and so formative to my life. The mementos in his study live up to their name – rich in value to their owner, many now looking forlorn as their purpose has passed.

There is my father's favourite painting of W. G. Grace curiously dressed as an Indian, there is the 'baggy green cap' from the 1960 Australian cricket tour which he used to pull down over my ears when I was a child, and a marvellously impish painting of him as a little boy at the age of five. Even then he had that twinkle which never left his eye.

The deep, overriding memory of my father is that of humour and kindness, hand in hand, accompanied by an almost subconscious principle of *doing the right thing*. He always taught us from an early age to treat people as *we* would like to be treated, to 'do as you would be done by', and in many respects this formed the moral basis of his life. The sadness stems not only from the loss of my father but more generally from the fact that we've *all* lost a very close friend, one to be thoroughly relied upon and trusted, one who had no hidden side. I am sure that much of his love for the game of cricket stemmed from his strong contention that, as he often said, people involved in the game are essentially *nice* people to be with; over the years he transmitted in every sense this belief in the goodness of the game to brilliant effect. He was – perhaps remarkably, given his provenance – a man to whom people from all backgrounds could relate. I never tired of the pride I felt at being by his side.

It's the humour, though, the constant laughter, that I'll always remember, the natural skill to see the funny side of almost any situation without malice. I only once remember him being silenced by a joke which backfired, in Adelaide for the 1979 Australia–England Women's Test match. He had been introducing me to all as 'my little boy' and as we entered the almost deserted ground he continued the joke between us by asking the ticket-seller, with a mischievous grin, for one-and-a-half tickets. These were duly given, and my father with a laugh gave them back and asked for two adult tickets instead. His mouth opened, then closed, when the answer came, 'No, you're right mate, it's full price for adults and half price for old age pensioners!'

I'll desperately miss the jokes, the family games, the gentle teasing, the regular telephone calls and the knowledge that he was always there. But he has left his family, and his family of friends, with the warmest thoughts and memories to keep us smiling – as he always did.

Lawrence Johnston

Lawrence Johnston, Johnners' nephew, recalls some outings with his 'Uncle Bri'.

Having lost my own father twenty years ago, and for more years than I can remember lived in Bri's house, my main reflection is that he was like a second father to me.

He was immensely generous, and I don't suppose he once forgot any of his many nephews or nieces at Christmas.

On the many occasions when my brother and I stayed with him in St John's Wood, at the end of our prep-school term in the fifties, we were invariably treated to at least two outings. We might attend a pantomime one day and a circus the next, with perhaps a radio show also thrown in.

On one occasion at Broadcasting House, his boss slapped him across the face. As a small eight-year-old in grey flannel shorts, I was extremely upset: 'How dare that man do that to my uncle who could do no wrong,' I boiled.

Had I been several years older, and been aware of my uncle's leg-pulling tendencies, I would have realized that it was merely a feigned slap made to appear realistic by the discreet clapping of his own hands at the apparent moment of impact.

The subtlety of that encounter may have been lost on one so little, but I have vivid memories of another bit of leg-pulling.

A prep-school pal called Tim Helps and I were taken by our headmaster Ted Aldrich-Blake (nickname A-B) to the Varsity match at Lord's.

Inside the commentary box, my uncle who was an old friend of A-B's got somebody to enter the box with a message saying that all four tyres of a Daimler bearing A-B's number plate had been let down. Bri read out the message, casually enquiring whether A-B knew who the owner was.

'Ohh! Those boys. You wait till we get back to school,' came the reply.

There was never a dull moment whenever Bri was around.

My brother and sisters and I loved that trick of his of tucking his ears in, something he was to treat chatshow audiences to in later years. And he had little catchphrases to convey his feelings, one of our favourite being 'Oh, my Crippen,' to show amazement.

His infectious enthusiasm and humour somehow rubbed off on those around him, and I am doubtless one of many folk who have made feeble attempts to copy his humour.

His fondness for nicknames went way beyond his famed 'ers' trademark. Mrs Winterbottom, who owned the Cornish boarding house where he holidayed with his family, was known as 'Mrs Summertop'.

And he was a great one for personalizing his enthusiasm. *Test Match Special* listeners often heard him enthusing about Nancy's lunches at Lord's. We in the family had a parallel. Whenever the name of Bri's aunt, Nancy Browning – Daphne du Maurier's mother-in-law – came up, Bri would eulogize about her cook Rose's meringues.

J. J. Warr

Brian was also a good neighbour according to John (J.J.) Warr, the Middlesex and England fast bowler who was to become president of the MCC.

The voice and the style of Johnners as a broadcaster always conveyed the image of a friendly neighbour. In the fifties and early sixties that was precisely what he was to me and my wife. He had a house in Cavendish Avenue, St John's Wood and we had a flat fifty yards away. We moved into the country in the sixties but he stayed faithful to St John's Wood, moving to a house in Hamilton Terrace and then to Boundary Road.

We laid some expensive carpets in our flat and our first visitors were two of the little Johnners wearing roller skates. They left with a flea in the ear. Paul McCartney, of Beatles fame, bought a house in Cavendish Avenue and had it extensively refurbished. The Johnners children decided to give it the once-over out of curiosity and set off the elaborate security alarms. They finished up in the St John's Wood nick and it required all of their father's legendary diplomatic skill to get them out with nothing more than a polite wigging.

Brian, at this time, was a BBC staff man and was given all sorts of bizarre assignments which he fulfilled with rare aplomb and enjoyment. It was characteristic of him that every day was fun and if the 'slings and arrows of outrageous fortune' ever came his way, he never showed it. He had a bright idea of a radio show to be called *Happy Families* which consisted of the Johnston family and the Warrs playing Christmassy-type parlour games on the air. Kenneth Horne was the MC and, after being recorded in Cavendish Avenue, it went out at 3 p.m. on Boxing Day. It had the lowest recorded listening figures in history and was scrapped immediately. Johnners and I did a music hall script, which he wrote, of the 'I say, I say, I say' variety which he so adored. I was paid eight guineas including expenses and I feel to this day that the BBC was robbed.

Whilst we did not live in each other's pockets, a visit to them or from them was always happy and full of laughs. Brian was still playing the odd cricket match at the time, keeping wicket and keeping his team highly amused.

One Sunday we went to a village to play the locals and Brian had invited 'Pom Pom' Fellowes-Smith, a South African Test player, to join us. It was an unwritten rule with Johnners that you did not score more than fifty or sixty if you were a batsman and you did not try to humiliate the opposition as a bowler. 'Pom Pom' knew nothing of this and went on well past fifty heading for a hundred. Johnners organized it that we all clapped when he got to ninety-something and, as the village only had a primitive scoreboard, 'Pom Pom' would not know his own total. We clapped, as did the crowd, 'Pom Pom' raised his cap, hit one more six to make sure and got out next ball. Then the score was put up. 'Last batsman 99.' Johnners was famous for getting the giggles and he certainly did that day.

Whilst the programme *Happy Families* flopped, my abiding memory of my neighbour is that of a very friendly one with a happy family and a tremendous zest for life.

13

CHARITY WORK

Brian Johnston was well known for his work for many charities but most notably for his support of the blind.

On every Saturday of a Test match, he would make an appeal on behalf of the Primary Club, pointing out the simple qualification for membership – to have been out first ball in any class of cricket. All they had to do then was send £10 to Mike Thomas, P.O. Box 111, Bromley, Kent to receive a tie (or, in the case of a lady, a brooch) and a membership certificate.

Mike Thomas is the honorary secretary of the Primary Club.

Mike Thomas

The Primary Club is a charity – registered number 285285 – whose aim is to supply sporting and recreational facilities for the visually impaired. Brian Johnston's concern for the blind is well known, and he did a great deal to help and support us. Many listeners to *Test Match Special* will know of the 'plug' he gave us on the Saturdays of home Test matches, but he was always encouraging behind the scenes as well. He used to let us know how appreciative he was of any help we gave to the Metropolitan Sports & Social Club for the Visually Handicapped (METRO), of which he was President. Blind cricket matches are happy occasions, but were made more special when Brian was there. His infectious enthusiasm communicated itself to players and spectators and made it all such fun.

Some of us were privileged to spend an afternoon with Brian during a function at Dorton House School for the Blind, Sevenoaks, and we saw at first hand his extraordinary courtesy and kindness to everyone he met. Many people wanted his autograph or to take a photograph of him, and each one was treated with the same cheerful consideration.

The Primary Club has been going for nearly forty years, and is run entirely by voluntary workers. We spend none of our funds on advertising and send out no mailshots apart from our annual newsletter to tell members what we are doing and to give them a statement of our accounts for the year, so Brian's efforts on our behalf were absolutely invaluable.

From the number of applications for membership we have received from all over the world, we know that many people from many countries listened to Brian on *Test Match Special* – some in preference to their own television commentaries! Letters we have had from Britain and from abroad show how much Brian was loved and respected by all cricket lovers, and through him we have gained many friends and supporters.

Mike Brace

Brian had a special relationship with the Metropolitan Sports and Social Club for the Visually Handicapped whose first chairman and now vice-president Mike Brace asked him to be their president in 1976.

Brian Johnston was much loved by everyone who met him but in the hearts of the members of the Metropolitan Sports and Social Club for the Visually handicapped, he had a very special place. Johnners, who seemed to give nicknames to those he came into contact with at the drop of a hat, was himself known within our club as 'the President'.

This takes very little explanation because that is what he was, our club's first and only president since our inauguration in April 1973. Brian often referred to us on air as his 'blind boys' and the support, encouragement and enjoyment Brian gave us was beyond measure.

Ironically, during the eighteen years Brian was our President many of Metro's members had never heard him give one of his legendary speeches other than on the radio. However, on Friday 26 November 1993, only a few days before his heart attack, he was the main speaker at our club's Twentieth Anniversary dinner at Lord's Cricket Ground. In November, Brian revealed for the first time that Metro was the first club to approach him to become its president and the first club which he had accepted. This is an immense source of pride to us all as Brian was a prize catch.

Metro was formed in 1973 by a group of young visually handicapped people who played cricket together regularly and wanted better organized sport with more opportunities and recognition. As the club grew in membership and range of sports undertaken, we began to look for a president who would take an interest in our activities, further the interests of blind cricket, and give the club an aspect of prestige associated with someone in the public eye. Brian fulfilled all of these aims many times over. For a man so busy in so many aspects of broadcasting, public speaking etc., he always found time for his club. Brian thought nothing of attending Metro's AGM and sitting with the twenty-five or so members that had turned up and, when appropriate, heckling the Committee (with everyone else). Again Brian, where possible, would turn up to watch one of our matches. These games, not played at Lord's or the Oval, were usually held at Highgate Wood in front of a crowd of about a dozen spectators who happened to be passing through the park at the time. This 'out-of-the-limelight' type of support and encouragement typifies the man who was our president.

I also remember very vividly being part of his persuasive devilment. In 1981 I received a phone call from Brian asking me to give a talk with him on the World Service about blind cricket. He said that he would arrange for a car to pick me up (a strange luxury for anyone who knows the World Service's budgetry constraints) and he asked me to wear something reasonable as we might have something to eat afterwards or go for a drink. I and the posh car duly turned up at the Strand to find Brian waiting for me and, much to my surprise, Eamonn Andrews and his little red book. I was to be the subject of *This Is Your Life* and Brian, the cunning devil, was the lure that had been used to get me there.

In the last five years Brian's unceasing work, with others, to get blind cricket taken seriously began to pay significant dividends. Metro has now given demonstrations at many first-class matches and Sunday League fixtures, and undertaken exhibitions of our adapted game at a number of Test matches including the exciting Sunday of the Lord's Test against Pakistan in 1992. Last year saw the final of the blind knockout competition (with Brian) at Lord's. Unfortunately Metro were not in the final but Brian, together with his friend the blind musician George Shearing, turned up to give his support and sense of fun to this occasion.

Brian's frequent mentions of the Primary Club brought in thousands of pounds for sports for blind children at a school in Kent and for blind sport in general. Brian was very insistent that all members should wear their ties on the Saturday of a Test match and I would like to see, in remembrance of Brian, that his name is linked to this ritual in future. I am sure it would have pleased Brian to think that his efforts would be continued.

The dinner at Lord's in November 1993 was the last time that any of us spoke to or were with Brian. Nearly 50 per cent of the club's members were there and Brian, the true professional and sparkling performer, delighted everyone with his charm, wit, and, there is no other word for it, 'niceness'. I will never forget that occasion and the man and all the goodness and fun which he stood for. If they have presidential suites in Heaven I am sure Johnners is booked in. He was much loved, and will be much missed by his 'blind boys' from Metro.

The young Johnners
– Brian with a
portrait of himself
as a boy
(Pauline Johnston).

The Prime Minister congratulating Brian on his eightieth birthday while
Pauline carries the bat presented by the Lord's Taverners *(The Lord's Taverners)*.

BJ surrounded by family portraits in the study of his
St John's Wood home *(Rex Features*/Sun).

Enjoying the game in the company of his old friend and fellow entertainer, Willie Rushton (*Allsport*).

Johnners wrestling with a tuba during the recording of the 1,500th edition of *Down Your Way* (BBC).

The *Test Match Special* team – left to right, Bill Frindall, Christopher Martin-Jenkins, Don Mosey, Fred Trueman, Tony Cozier, BJ, Trevor Bailey, Jonathan Agnew, Vic Marks, Peter Baxter and Mike Selvey *(BBC)*.

The *Down Your Way* team – Brian Martin, BJ, Chris Stevens and Anthony Smith *(BBC)*.

Relaxing on holiday in the early 1960s with children Clare, Ian, Barry and Andrew *(Pauline Johnston)*.

Brian with his daughter, Joanna, when she presented flowers to Barbara Cartland at the opening of Little Berkhamsted Cricket Club's new pavilion in 1977 *(Pauline Johnston)*.

Behind every great man... Pauline and Brian (*Rex Features*).

Johnners in his second home – the commentary box at Lord's in 1991
(*Patrick Eagar*).

Sidney Fielden

Wherever he went, Brian would carry out little acts of kindness which often went unnoticed – but not by people like Sidney Fielden, chairman of Yorkshire's public relations and membership committee.

Whenever Brian came to Headingley, he made a special effort to see two of our members, Anthony and Paul Sollitt, brothers in their mid-forties who live in York. Both have been blind since the age of six.

They have been Yorkshire members for many years, along with their late mother, Mrs Jean Sollitt, who died of cancer at the end of the 1991 season. And Brian knew them well.

I can remember the last time he came from the commentary position to where I was with them in front of the dressing rooms. He spent half an hour with them and was his usual kind and sympathetic self.

Later in the day, he mentioned the two brothers on *Test Match Special*. It meant a great deal to them.

Tony Swainson

Another charity close to Brian's heart was the Lord's Taverners, and Capt. Tony Swainson, OBE, RN, Director for twenty years, pays tribute to his untiring efforts on their behalf.

The professional white man. I first met Brian at the Lord's Taverners twenty-first anniversary ball at the Grosvenor House, London, in November 1971, when my wife and I were guests of Neil Durden-Smith and his wife, Judith Chalmers. I had known Neil ten years earlier when we were both serving in the Royal Navy.

Brian was the 160th member to join the Lord's Taverners, who were formed in 1950 by Martin Boddey, an opera singer turned actor. Early members included such well-known names as Sir John Barbirolli, John Snagge, John Arlott, Jack Hobbs, John Mills, Billy Griffith, Terence Rattigan, Richard Attenborough, Jack Hawkins and Richard Burton. The charity's first president was John Mills, and Prince Philip, the Duke of Edinburgh, accepted the office of 'Twelfth Man'. HRH has held this position to this day and his youngest son, Prince Edward, is the current president.

In 1962, Leslie Frewin edited a Lord's Taverner miscellany of cricket, entitled *The Boundary Book*. Johnners contributed a typical article full of stories and anecdotes. One such story inevitably concerned Freddie Trueman.

Brian wrote: 'One of Yorkshire's pre-season matches was against York. Freddie soon got among the wickets, bowling with surprising speed and ferocity so early in the season. He had taken his first five wickets and the next batsman emerged from the pavilion. He was an upright, military figure with a bristling white moustache and an I Zingari cap. The sleeves of his silk, cream shirt were buttoned to the wrists and he had on a pair of those skeleton pads which used to be fashionable in the days of W. G. Grace. He was an imposing sight but, under-standably enough, he looked a trifle apprehensive at what he was about to face.

'The Yorkshire captain saw him coming, and, realizing the county were doing a bit too well, went up to Freddie and said: "This is Brigadier X. He is an important member of the county. Let him get a few."

'So Freddie, in his most affable and friendly manner, went up to the batsman as he approached the wicket and said: "Good morning, Brigadier. With my first ball I shall give you one to get off the mark." The brigadier looked greatly relieved but his expression soon changed as Freddie went on: "Aye, and with my second I'll pin you against the flippin' sightscreen!" ' A typical Johnners story.

Johnners' schoolboy humour is well recorded but he had one other passion on the humour front – seaside postcards. I invariably had the pleasure of receiving such a card from Brian when he was on holiday.

Whenever the Lord's Taverners had a cricket match on a Sunday I used to send Brian details of the game and he never failed to mention it in his *Test Match Special* broadcasts.

The programme has now passed into the folklore of the land with Brian Johnston as the helm. His view of it was 'just a bunch of friends overheard at a cricket match.' Cricket is, of course, the ideal sport for radio commentary. Its pace, history and aesthetic qualities make it that. All over the cricketing world small boys sit at matches imagining themselves to be a Brian Johnston talking through an over.

As Peter Baxter, the producer, described: 'One spring evening in 1984, with the scent of new-mown grass and linseed oil hinting at the birth of a new season, four of the *Test Match Special* team met at the Royal Garden Hotel for dinner. Over the port, they relived, with the help of the BBC archives, some great moments. Great deeds by men from Bradman to Botham were recalled – the winning of the Ashes in 1953, 1971 and 1977. Brian Johnston, doyen of the team as the BBC's first cricket correspondent and a man who aims to put back some of the pleasure which the game has given him over the years, led the conversation. Together with Trevor Bailey, Fred Trueman and Christopher Martin-Jenkins, and an introduction by John Arlott, they produced a recording which was sold to benefit the Lord's Taverners.'

Terry Wogan was then president of the Lord's Taverners and he wrote: 'The great days of the "wireless" were before the Great God Television took hold of the eyeballs of the great British public. And yet and yet, radio continues to weave its spell to hold the attention and imagination of millions of faithful daily listeners. What better example of this than the BBC's *Test Match Special* team who so brilliantly convey to millions, not only in Britain but worldwide, the atmosphere, the colour and the flavour of a Test match.

'You don't have to know a thing about cricket to dwell on and savour the soothing tones, the rolling phrases, the gentle nuances of Johnston, Arlott, Bailey, Trueman, Blofeld, Martin-Jenkins, Lewis, Frindall and the rest of the merry band. Their contribution to entertainment is as great as it is to cricket. My thanks to the *Test Match Special* team and their producer, Peter Baxter, not just for the past enjoyment they have given but also in allowing the Lord's Taverners to benefit from their recollections and fascinating archive material.'

The prime mover in all this was dear old Johnners. The Lord's Taverners' *Best of Test Match Special* was a great success and raised a considerable amount of money for our charity.

In 1981, we sounded out Brian with a view to his taking over the presidency in 1982. Alas, although he was highly honoured to be invited, he had to decline owing to pressure of work. Brian was tireless in undertaking speaking engagements for us all over the country as well as taking part in our cabaret promotions – and, on one occasion, even a wine-tasting competition.

Brian, who knew the Taverners from its formative years, found difficulty in accepting our more commercial approach in the 1970s. But when he saw what the additional grant aid was able to achieve, including buses for handicapped children, I think he withdrew his earlier reservations. Remember, in the earlier days, the Lord's Taverners was a fun organization with little appreciation of its charitable potential. In 1972, they were raising £18,000 per annum as against £1.5 million at the end of the eighties.

Lord's Taverners no. 160 will be sadly missed by us all.

Heather Ewart

Brian was a patron of the Handicapped Adventure Playground Association for seventeen years. Their vice-chairman, Mrs Heather Ewart, remembers 'a professional to the last degree, punctual, punctilious, informal and friendly.'

We first met Brian in 1977 through the then producer of Charity Appeals at the BBC. The first HAPA playground in Chelsea was an immediate success and by 1977 three other special playgrounds had opened for disabled children in London which were packed with children every day. But development brings expense and the chance to make a charity appeal was heaven-sent. Brian Johnston became our guardian angel and willingly agreed to make the radio appeal on our behalf. He went to see the Hayward Playground in Islington and spent a great deal of time there, talking to the staff and watching the children who, whatever their disability, were enjoying all the challenge and fun of the playground, playing inside the building and out of doors. He was particularly impressed by the dedication of the playstaff and mentioned each one by name in his broadcast. And of course he was right. Without the staff we could not care for so many children, all with differing abilities or give them the opportunity for play and fun and friendship which is our aim. Then and there Brian agreed to become a patron of HAPA.

In the years following, HAPA's work expanded and money was important if we were to maintain our five adventure playgrounds, the National Information Service and the other strands of our work. In 1992, with the opportunity to make another radio appeal Brian again agreed to help us. And again he could not have been more helpful with his quick understanding, sympathy and with his own touches which made the appeal so successful. But it is not just for his help with our appeals that we are grateful. He was in touch with us, taking an interest in the playgrounds and keeping abreast of new developments in the welfare of disabled children. He was a firm friend.

We hope that this book of anecdotes and memories of Brian will bring a smile to many and that his generous help to HAPA and other charities will be remembered too.

Paul Russell from From Brisbane to Karachi *(Queen Anne Press)*

14

THE ENTERTAINER

Mike Craig

'A smile, a song and a love of variety' – Mike Craig, comedy writer, BBC Light Entertainment Radio producer and Scribe Rat of the Grand Order of Water Rats, remembers Johnners, the entertainer who just loved to be entertained.

I realized I'd forgotten the microphone stand just as the taxi turned into Boundary Road. 'Oh dear,' thought I, 'what will this distinguished broadcaster think of this Yorkshire erk from the Beeb in Manchester?' I could hear the thoughts going through his mind as I apologized – 'All this modern equipment and he's forgotten the mike stand, huh, they don't make BBC producers like they used to!' But, no. He just laughed. 'No problem,' he said. 'We'll improvise.' We did. With the aid of five or six editions of Wisden, two elastic bands, some sellotape, a rolled-up newspaper and a bull-dog clip we made one of the best table microphone stands ever used in the history of broadcasting. Blue Peter would have been proud of us! We recorded the programme – *It's a Funny Business, ask Brian*

Johnston – which contained the stories, the embarrassing moments and the gaffes, all of which are now so familiar to us. I dismantled the makeshift mike stand and another 'gem' was in the can. He took me to The Tavern (the pub next door to the Grace Gates) for lunch and a friendship was forged over sausage and mash. Johnners and Craigers were an item!

That was in 1977. I *first* met Brian when I was twelve years old. Like millions of others I was introduced to him by my best friend – the wireless. As Eric Coates' 'Knightsbridge March' heralded the weekly edition of *In Town Tonight* my senses would tingle. (The wireless had that effect on people my age.) 'Get your violets, dear, lovely violets,' cried Mrs Baker every week, battling vocally in Piccadilly Circus against 'the mighty roar of London's traffic', which was stopped on cue every Saturday night at 7.30 p.m. Brian's spot on the show was the best. He was cast superbly. The programme's intrepid adventurer. The Indiana Jones of his day! His section was called 'Let's go somewhere'. You name it, Brian did it. He did it 'live' with a youthful enthusiasm which, thank goodness, never left him. He rode pillion on a stunt man's motor bike as he crashed through flaming barrels, he lay down in an inspection pit between railway lines as an express hurtled over him, he was shaved on stage by the Crazy Gang, he 'busked' in the street outside a theatre queue, and he sang 'Underneath the Arches' with his idol Bud Flanagan outside the Victoria Palace, Johnners himself playing the street piano (the only tune he could play). That above anything else he ever did, and he did a lot, was his proudest broadcasting moment.

Johnners and Craigers shared a real love of that wonderful era when live entertainment was 'twice nightly' in hundreds of theatres across the land. Mums, dads and kids could all enjoy and afford traditional British Variety. For Brian, 'Wilson, Keppel and Betty' were as appealing as 'Worrell, Walcott and Weekes'. Before he admired Keith Miller he'd adored Max. Joan Rhodes couldn't deceive a batsman with the flight of a cricket ball, but Wilfred Rhodes couldn't tear a London telephone directory in half. (Well if he could, he never said 'owt!)

Not only did he love watching these greats on stage, he longed to be up there with them. I rang him once and asked him if he'd be interested in playing himself in the radio programme I co-wrote called *The Enchanting World of Hinge and Bracket*. I told him that I'd had an idea that *Down Your Way* could come to Stackton Tressle, the village where the 'ladies' lived. Brian bit my hand off to get writing! The result was a hilarious episode with Brian in and among the laughs, timing his lines to perfection like the best of them (and not having to wear a frock).

He was a frustrated 'one half of a double act'.

JOHNNERS   My dog's got no nose.
BEN WARRISS   How does it smell?
JOHNNERS   Terrible!
Collapse of audience.
Blackout.

Over the last five or six years it has been a tradition that Johnners, Craigers and Suers (my wife Susan) would meet at my house the Saturday night of the Old Trafford Test (Old Trafford being two and a half miles from my house). The procedure was that I would pick him up at The Swan at Bucklow Hill and bring him home to dinner (simple, plain English food, by order). Afterwards we would retire to the lounge for the entertainment.

'What have you got lined up for me tonight, Craigers?'

'Robb Wilton, Sandy Powell, Ted Ray, Jimmy Wheeler and Morris and Cowley.'

'Marvellous.'

He was in seventh heaven as the classic videos rolled before him. The following year I played him Freddie Frinton performing that brilliant piece of comedy, *Dinner for One*. I can see Brian now wiping the tears from his eyes at the display of Freddie Frinton's drunken genius.

The most memorable night of all was a couple of years ago. I had a real surprise in store for him. He sat in the armchair, I pressed the button and on to the screen came a video of the final night of the very last *Crazy Gang Show* from the Victoria Palace. He was in another world as the corny jokes flew across the footlights, as the cheeky sketches and 'cross-overs' were re-born in front of him.

Teddy Knox is on stage. He is interrupted by Monsewer Eddie Gray who is carrying a large carton of what appears to be a pyramid of very large snooker balls.

KNOX What have you got there?

MONSEWER My latest work of art.

KNOX That's a picture of a snooker set.

MONSEWER No it isn't. It's a picture of Jayne Mansfield hiding in a pile of grapefruit!

Schoolboy humour you say? Yes, but he loved it. You see, that was Johnners!

When the show ended he was speechless. By the miracle of video and a good TV producer friend of mine who got me the tape, Brian had been able to see again all that he loved and cherished in entertainment. I took the cassette out of the machine and delivered the line I'd been saving up for weeks: 'Oh, by the way Johnners – this is for you!' I gave him the tape. He couldn't have looked happier if he'd just stumped Bradman first ball!

He told me since that the bit he enjoyed watching again and again was when the elderly Bud Flanagan came to the footlights and said he couldn't sing 'Underneath the Arches' without Chesney Allen. 'Come on Ches,' he calls, and a 'not very well' Chesney Allen climbed on to the stage, joined his old partner and they did it for the last time. I'll never forget the expression on Johnners' face that night at my house. It was a mixture of emotions. Almost in tears at the sight and sound of this irreplaceable pair, yet with a slight look of envy.

I really do believe that in a perfect world for Brian, it would have been 'Flanagan and Johnners'.

Saturday nights after an Old Trafford Test will never be the same.

Lord Rix

Brian Johnston was, by his own admission, stage-struck from a very early age, so much so that when he returned to civilian life after the war his original intention was to be an actor or, failing that, go into the management or production side of the business.

He never actually fulfilled that ambition but, as luck would have it, he joined the BBC Outside Broadcast Department where one of his first jobs was to broadcast live from theatres and music halls all over the country. Brian – now Lord – Rix remembers him well.

'I'm sure nobody walks much faster than I do!'
'He can't do that,' said the King,
'or else he'd have been here first.'
(Lewis Carroll)
What's more, Johnners would've been!

The very first excerpt from a West End play was televised by the BBC on 14 May 1952. It was the first act of my first presentation at the Whitehall Theatre, *Reluctant Heroes*, and the man they chose to make the first introduction was a man used to being first at many things – Brian Johnston.

I first met him on the afternoon of the transmission – live in those days – and was charmed by his good nature and the ease with which he approached the task ahead – second-nature to him, but desperately important to me, for my future as a successful actor-manager in farce rested on those fateful forty minutes, beginning at 9.20 p.m., and his introduction would either enthuse the viewers or otherwise.

I needn't have worried. The theatre audience were raring to go; Brian pumped up their adrenalin even more; then – as we went on air – turned his attention to the audience at home, who promptly fell out of their sofas and chairs in riotous abandon at our antics and, when it was all over at ten o'clock, the Box Office 'phones started ringing and never really stopped for the next fifteen years. Whitehall farce had come to stay.

My view of Johnners? Definitely the man to have on your side and go in first. An opening bat of the highest order, with a wide range of strokes and still worth his place in the team until the very day he died. There aren't many like that . . .

Willie Rushton

Among those listening to those early broadcasts was the famed humourist Willie Rushton who was to join Johnners behind the microphone.

In all honesty I couldn't tell you when I first met Johnners. He was one of those people you were born knowing. I certainly didn't know him when I first heard him on the radio, commentating from under some London stage on the activities of a conjurer above – 'My word, now he's sawing her in half!' (*sawing noises*) – or some slapstick from Lupino Lane and his relations – 'Now he's running across the stage with a bucket of custard! (*the thump! thump! thump! of comedy boots, a splash, audience hilarity*) My word! That *was* funny!'

I think that the first time I met him was on perhaps the only occasion that he tasted unpopularity. Some time in the seventies (it's not a recent phenomenon) BBC Radio decided that Change is for the Better. This time they decided to change the cast of the long-running and highly successful *Twenty Questions*, except for Anona Winn, who was beyond Change. Terry Wogan was put in the Chair. The new team consisted of a very beautiful Belgian lady with a hint of the Gabors, and myself, under the impression that I was signing up for *What's My Line?* and seeing myself as a new Gilbert Harding. Well, aspects of Gilbert. Pause for true story. A young Oxford blue, he opened the batting and kept wicket, was asked how a charity match in Vincent's Square had gone. 'Not well,' he replied,

'I batted Number Eleven, fielded in the deep, and was importuned in the lavatories by Gilbert Harding.' Johnners always enjoyed that one. Back to the plot. The last member of the team was Johnners who was replacing a much-loved baggy-nosed comic, who had for years understudied the entire Crazy Gang, and entered the hearts of millions via *Jackanory*.

The rest of us got away with it. Not so poor Johnners. For some months he became the recipient of vicious hate-mail. As vicious as only the British middle-classes can get when they don't get their ball back.

Otherwise we met at various cricket matches, both frivolous and serious, and always laughed a lot. The most enjoyable interview I ever had was with Johnners at the Oval in 1986. He used to conduct them during the luncheon interval on Test match Saturdays. 'Chats' he called them, and I've never bumped into anyone with whom he 'chatted' who didn't remember the twenty minutes or so as pure joy. And then there was *Test Match Trivia* which ran for the last ten years, much to the surprise of Johnners, Tim Rice and I. Its longevity was largely due, I'd say, to Old Johnners' benign but sharp chairmanship. It was something he'd never tackled previously, but I don't think it occurred to anyone for a moment that he wouldn't make a success of it. I would like to hear again the second show we recorded at Windsor Cricket Club. Usually the ladies provided refreshment and vol-au-vents after we'd recorded the two programmes. On this particular night drinks were brought out *between* the two programmes and it's fair to say that Johnners overdid it. Heavens above, it was a convivial soirée and everyone was always so glad to see him and talk to him and there are times when it's hard to say 'No,' but there were consonants to come and words like 'sarsaparilla'. Bill Tidy was there and Tim Brooke-Taylor (Johnners had to call him 'Brookers') and Rice and I and none of us have ever laughed as loud. It would have to be the unedited version I'd like to listen to, as by the time it emerged from Radio 4 with retakes and the necessary scissors it probably sounded quite within the bounds. Suffice to say that Old Johnners was a very funny man.

I was in Australia when I heard of his death and the *Daily Telegraph* asked for a few lines and I faxed them the following and I don't know whether it ever saw the light of day but it came from the heart.

'I never knew anybody who enjoyed life so much and shared that enjoyment so effortlessly and so unselfishly. How we'll miss him. He was summer. He was cricket. He was England. I hope someone checks on the health of the Ravens at the Tower and the Gibbons on the Rock. Wherever you are, Johnners, there will surely be cake. Love, Rushers.'

Roy Hudd

Comedian Roy Hudd, who shared Brian's love of music hall, has his own special memory of Johnners.

A few years back Brian took part in a re-creation of radio's *In Town Tonight*. His adventures on that programme became legendary and one of his fondest memories, of the original programme, was interviewing Bud Flanagan and the Crazy Gang. Indeed he was grabbed by the Gang and dragged onstage during a performance at the Victoria Palace. Once there he was pushed into a barber's chair and lathered and shaved by Bud and his evil crew – all 'live'.

For the re-creation, Brian had the idea of interviewing yours truly 'live' at the Prince of Wales theatre where I was playing Bud in *Underneath the Arches*. Brian was in my dressing room as Broadcasting House came over to him but I was still onstage (I must have got a laugh that night!). Ever the trooper, Brian conducted an in-depth interview with my son – who was dressing me in his school holidays! He kept all the balls in the air until I finally arrived. We had just enough time to say hello and for me to place an enormous custard pie in the Johnners clock. As he had to travel, in a rickshaw, up Regent Street to Broadcasting House (don't ask me why!) I thought it would be fun *and* a reminder of his heroes.

I cherish the sound of the custard-dripping Johnston voice floating up to the dressing room from Piccadilly Circus – 'Both you Hudders are rotters!'

Leslie Crowther

Comedian Leslie Crowther, who was seriously injured in a car crash in 1992, has fond memories of Brian's passion for music hall – and the time he was grateful for it.

Brian Johnston had a great love of music hall and his cup of joy overflowed when he sang 'Underneath the Arches' with me as Flanagan and Allen. It shone in his eyes, the sheer enjoyment of it all in making his share of involvement in music hall so complete. And I felt privileged to have done it with him.

Brian especially loved that saucy humour known around the world as 'honest music hall vulgarity', several postcards of the seaside variety falling into this category. He would delight in sending them to his friends . . . and he wouldn't deliberate which! Unlike me. When I had the courage to send him an extremely offensive postcard from France, I put it under a sealed cover. Not that it would have mattered – the writing was in French!

Anyway, the fact of the matter is that it all helped towards my recovery from my accident, for which, dear Brian, I thank you.

Fitzpatrick, Bamforth & Co. Ltd

Sir Peter Saunders

Brian simply loved the company of actors and actresses and one man who gave him plenty of opportunities to rub shoulders with them was Sir Peter Saunders, theatrical impresario and producer of more than 150 shows, including the world record-breaking The Mousetrap. *Yet Sir Peter fondly remembers Johnners for a quite different reason.*

Brian was, to use an out-moded word, a gentleman. And one in every sense of the word. In the forty plus years I have known him, I have never heard anyone say a single word against him. Or, incidentally, vice versa. And I don't think anyone would want a better epitaph than that.

But he was the perennial schoolboy. When car telephones were introduced to this country, they started off with only 369 'channels'. In other words, only 369 people in the country had car telephones and I happened to get one.

I gave Brian a lift home from Lord's one day. He saw this rather bulky microphone attached to the dashboard, and was intrigued to know what it was. 'How does it work?' 'How do you use it?' I explained you got through to the number, pressed while you spoke and released the button when you listened (or was it the other way round?), and had to remember to say 'Roger' when you had finished talking because it was one-way transmission.

Brian was fascinated. We were outside his home. Could he give Pauline a ring? Of course. He was like a boy with a new train. He spoke to Pauline and rather proudly remembered to finish up with 'Roger And Out.'

Then he asked was it possible to go into the house and telephone me in the car from home. Certainly. So he dashed in and after our talk triumphantly ended with 'Roger And Out.' He told me later he got almost – yes, almost – as much fun out of using that phone as he did watching a Compton century.

Dear Brian. If my wife, Katie, is right, you will still be able to get through to us from where you are. So Roger – but not 'out'.

15

THE SPEAKER

'Dabber' Davis

'Dabber' Davis and his wife, Paddy, who launched Brian on to the after-dinner speaking circuit, and to whom he was unfailingly loyal, were proud of their famous client.

Brian Johnston was, as everyone knows, the king of the after-dinner speakers, and as we represented him in this field for nearly thirty years there are many stories, but none that illustrate the point that whoever is making the introduction should remember the words of the great Lord Birkett on introducing anyone: 'Stand Up, Speak Up and Shut Up.'

At one multi-national dinner a very pompous Company Chairman stood up to introduce Brian, their Guest Celebrity Speaker, and to everyone's amazement he proceeded to read an entire CV on Brian – from his schooldays, holidays, going up to Eton and Oxford, entering the family coffee business prior to joining the Guards, and subsequently going through many of the famous battle campaigns, ending up with the Military Cross for bravery. At the end of the war, being demobbed, joining the

BBC, covering every television and broadcasting event you can think of, quite apart from the world of cricket, i.e. Royal funerals, Coronations, *In Town Tonight*, Variety Theatre visits, circus and West End musical broadcasts etc., etc., etc. In other words, this pompous windbag droned on and on, obviously wanting to give the impression that he knew Brian intimately and was an old friend, which he obviously wasn't!

Finally, as the Chairman was nearing the end of his diatribe, which had lasted practically fifteen minutes, he said, 'And in conclusion, as a special treat, I am sure at the end of his speech we can prevail on Brian to sing us a couple of choruses of his award-winning song 'Looking high high high, looking low low low'. (As many will know, *Bryan Johnson* had – a few years previously – won the Eurovision Song Contest for the UK with this song.)

It is quite remarkable to remember the enormous range of Brian's radio work over the last forty years or so, and although foremost in everyone's mind, obviously, were the cricket commentaries and *Down Your Way*, many will remember the brilliant 'Let's Go Somewhere' section of the old *In Town Tonight* series where Brian went everywhere and anywhere, lying under express trains, pillion riding with daredevil motorcyclists, busking, dressed as a tramp, to see how generous the public were, and, something he loved so much, interviewing film, stage and radio stars in their dressing rooms.

It was on one of these visits to the No. 1 Dressing Room at the London Palladium that Brian met the famous American film star, Jimmy 'Schnozzle' Durante. After the very successful interview, they were having a drink and chatting amicably, when Brian said to Jimmy Durante, 'You know, Jimmy, apart from our love of show business, we have something else in common – we both have large noses!' To which Jimmy Durante replied, in his own inimitable way, 'Brian, *dat's* not a schnozz, that's just a baby!' and then pointing to his own nose he said, '*Dis* is a schnozz, a veritable mark of distinction!'

Raymond Gubbay

Brian was well into his seventies when Raymond Gubbay, the theatrical agent, proposed an entirely new venture. Johnners jumped at the chance.

'Lovely idea, let's do it,' was the characteristic response when I approached Brian Johnston to do an afternoon show about cricket. I had wanted something non-musical to act as a foil to the full round of seasonal music in my Christmas festival at the Barbican. And so on 27 December 1983 at three o'clock in the afternoon, 'That's Cricket' was born in front of 1,600 people in the City of London. Johnners started the show in characteristic form, 'I'm wearing my Raymond Gubbay suit,' he said, 'small checks,' before announcing that there were only 123 days left before Fenners and the start of the new season.

His 'team' that afternoon consisted of Jim Swanton, Tony Lewis and Ian Wallace, and Johnners led them on a leisurely discussion accompanied by suitable archive film. It was so successful that we decided to take it on tour – Manchester, Leeds, Northampton, Cardiff, Canterbury, Bournemouth and dozens of other places – we covered the cricket-loving areas of the country. Johnners' side changed from place to place but Jim Laker and Tom Graveney provided the backbone of support. We travelled about in a mini-coach fitted with aircraft-type reclining seats, and we always carried much food and drink. After a while, Johnners would suggest we open the 'Muscers' (Muscadet) and make a start on the 'Smokers' (smoked salmon sandwiches). A jolly crew arrived at the destination, the food and drink were transferred backstage and a first-class show always followed.

I knew I had become a real part of the team when at lunch one day with Jim Laker and myself, Brian turned to Jim and said, 'Well Gubbers says we ought to do so-and-so,' and so it was Gubbers evermore. We returned to the Barbican most Christmases, a summer brightness descending for a couple of hours over the City. Johnners was always in glowing form, full of enthusiasm and vigour; he was incapable of ever giving a dull performance.

I last saw him in the summer when he asked me to lunch with George Shearing and his wife. He was in the middle of his one-man-show tour and was particularly thrilled that he had filled the Chichester Festival Theatre to capacity. I wanted to ask him whether he had been on a share of the box-office rather than taking just a straight fee so I said, 'Were you on sharers, Johnners?' 'Should've been, Gubbers, shouldn't I?'

Richard Stilgoe

Brian shared many a stage with his old friend Richard Stilgoe, whom he once described as 'simply the best cabaret artist of the present day – a pianist, singer, lyricist, composer, teller of jokes and outrageous puns.'

But he winced a little at the references to his age when Richard composed this song for their appearance together on one of Harry Secombe's Highway *programmes from Broadhalfpenny Down, Hambledon, renowned as the cradle of cricket.*

It All Began At Hambledon

At Hambledon, upon this spot, high up on Hampshire's chalk,
A million trillion years ago, the dinosaurs did walk.
The great Gattingosauruses – short-legged with thick necks,
That fearsome giant carnivore, Bothamosaurus Rex.
Across this very turf they strode – one short and fat, one tall –
And came across an ancient pub they call the Bat and Ball.
Declared Gattingosaurus – 'There's a field and a pub,
It's the Ice Age and it's raining – we should start a cricket club.'

So it all began at Hambledon, a billion years ago –
Brian Johnston saw it, and Brian ought to know.

Bothamosaurus Rex then found a Pterodactyl's egg,
And rubbed it on his scaly tail, so it would swing to leg.
He went and pulled three trees up from a nearby Hampshire
  thicket
And cried 'Look Gatt – the wheel!' Gatt said 'Rubbish that's a
  wicket.'
And then Gattingosaurus found a club of slate so vast,
So long and wide from side to side that no ball could get past.
Bothamosaurus Rex then took the obvious revenge,
And made the wickets bigger – which is how we get Stonehenge.

  Yes it all took place at Hambledon, as the world began to
  wake,
  And Brian Johnston watched while eating prehistoric cake.

They batted through the Stone Age, the scores became colossal,
Boycottodon was in so long he turned into a fossil.
They said 'If only we had Hickthyosaurus in the side.
But he hasn't been here long enough, and isn't qualified.'

Eventually the dinosaurs of Hambledon got sent
A letter postmarked London (which was forwarded from Kent)
'The Mammoth Cricket Club (that is the MCC to you)
Is happy to inform you that your membership's come through.'
And so the dinosaurs marched off to London in their hordes
They're not extinct at all – they're all alive and well at Lord's.
They sleep in the pavilion, dreaming neolithic dreams
And ev'ry now and then wake up, and pick the England team.

  But it all began at Hambledon – it did – I do declare –
  Brian Johnston told me, and he knows, 'cos he was there.

16

W.G. AND KIPPER

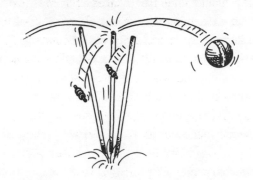

As everyone knows, Brian Johnston was a man of many parts but did you know that he once had shares in a racehorse and a greyhound, tried to make a hit record and helped in the revival of country-house cricket?

The men in the know were David Brown, the former Warwickshire and England fast bowler who now runs a stud farm with his wife, Trisha; Michael Melford, distinguished former cricket correspondent of the Daily Telegraph; *band-leader Vic Lewis; and well known cricket benefactor J. Paul Getty.*

David Brown

I was lucky enough to play my cricket and make all my overseas tours during the Johnners era and without doubt he made all the tours more enjoyable to be on. His sense of fun was invaluable and he was responsible for boosting morale on several trips.

It was on the 1968 tour to the West Indies that I met my future wife

Trish who was riding as a jockey on the flat in Jamaica. Trish and I became good friends with Brian and Pauline, and Johnners was unlucky enough to come and stay with us when we were in the process of syndicating a yearling racehorse colt among a group of friends. After a drink or two Brian decided that as long as his very good friend Sir Martin Gilliat, racing manager and private secretary to the Queen Mother, thought it was a good idea they would take two shares. Sir Martin readily agreed and Johnners set about naming the beast. He was sired by a stallion called Grey Mirage and our man could not resist connecting 'Grey' and Grace and the horse duly became 'W.G.Greys'. This name actually appeared on a bookmaker's cheque when, after he ran and won at Teesside Park, yours truly celebrated so long that the bookmakers had gone home when I went to collect. I therefore wrote to the bookie for my winnings and received a cheque made out to W.G. Greys!

W.G. won two races for us and gave us great fun. I remember him running at Newbury one day and as Trish and I walked towards the saddling boxes we heard that wonderful hunting horn impersonation and there, of course, were the unmistakable brown and white shoes and ample nose of B.A.J. While waiting to enter the parade ring Johnners informed us that if the horse caused any problems we would be perfectly safe as he was at Eton with two of the stewards and in the Guards with the other two!

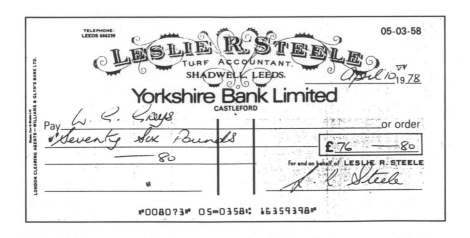

Unfortunately he did not run well enough to make any abuse of the rules possible. In the parade ring our trainer, Reg Hollmshead, introduced Brian to Frank Marby who was to ride W.G. 'Tell me Frank, what do you think of our horse?' asked Johnners. 'Well guv'nor,' replied Frank, 'I rode against him at Chester last month and I saw his arse for two furlongs and then went past so quickly that I didn't get much of a look at him!'

On the occasion Frank mentioned at Chester, B.A.J., Bob Willis and myself had all driven across from Scarborough where Warwickshire had been playing in the Fenner Trophy. We arrived early enough for Brian to order Chablis and smoked salmon which put us in a good frame of mind to attack the bookies. As you may guess Bob and Brian stood out just a little and perhaps, as they approached the bookmaker, he thought the owners were going for a coup! Anyway, he rubbed W.G.'s price off the board and I suddenly heard Johnners' unmistakable tones. 'I'll have you reported to the Jockey Club, my man. I have lots of friends in Portman Square.' Of course, the assembled crowd thought it was marvellous!

One other racing memory of Brian was when W.G. ran at Newmarket and we quite fancied him. However, he ran an absolute stinker and I was just licking my betting wounds when I bumped into Johnners. 'Terrible Brian, wasn't it?' said I. 'Well, I was a bit disappointed until I bumped into a friend of mine who had just had his first winner after owning horses for thirty years so I suppose we are lucky.'

It was impossible to be downhearted in his company and he turned quite a few days at the races into days of complete entertainment. He will be missed in the racing fraternity.

Michael Melford

One never ceased to marvel at Brian's capacity to raise people's spirits. There was the kindness which prompted his telephone calls to ailing friends or to friends who he had not seen recently. There was his manipulation of the English language which turned complete strangers

into contributors in the world of Johnston. My wife remembers a Mr
Coombs who, after his initial surprise, revelled in being addressed as
Catters. There was the wine waiter in Australia with horn-rimmed glasses
who responded no less swiftly to being called Horners.

One might have thought that there were cases when the humourless
or the stuffy might have seen such familiarity as in poor taste or an affront
to their dignity, but if there were, I do not remember them. Brian must
have had some hidden sensitivity which told him how far he could go.

There was also that trumpeting noise with which Brian would announce
himself. On one of the England tours of Pakistan which clashed with
political demonstrations and riots, the England team and the Press party
were confined to the Intercontinental Hotel in Lahore and relieved the
boredom by going round and round the nine-hole pitch-and-putt course
in the grounds. It was known that Johnston was due to arrive before
the first Test but when the human trumpet sounded from the steps of
the hotel, the words 'Johnners is here,' could be heard from all quarters
and everyone seemed to cheer up.

That tour ended when the Test match in Karachi was abandoned on
the third morning through communal riots. The Press and broadcasters were collected in what had recently been the England dressing-
room and were shepherded, all of us, into a small and far-from-new
saloon car. Johnston was the last in and those of us underneath him
were kept informed of our progress by his commentary from near the
roof.

Unlike many extroverts of similar humour he was quick to appreciate
other human beings and their contributions to the community. Hence the
perfect casting of him to present *Down Your Way*. On one occasion in
Tasmania I drove him from Hobart to Launceston on the first morning of a match. We stopped briefly outside the hotel to check in and
leave our baggage. When we came out, I had been given a parking
ticket.

Next morning Brian insisted on accompanying me to the police station
where we revealed ourselves as travellers from a far country and expressed our dismay at having infringed the law. The young policeman at
the desk took the ticket and disappeared into an inner sanctum to consult
a higher authority. After a few minutes he returned with the words 'She's

right.' Brian was charmed with them and never forgot them. It must have been no less memorable a meeting for the young policeman who can never have met anyone like Brian before.

There was a period in the sixties when Brian's enthusiasm extended to greyhound racing. He may not have been a fervent follower of it but when the call came from Colin Cowdrey for him to take a quarter share in a dog called Kentish Kipper, which was about to go into business at Catford, he did not refuse. The other two shares were held by John Woodcock and myself.

The Kipper did win once or twice, though not often when the connections were present. The one certainty about him was that if there was any bumping at the first bend, he would be the one who was put out of the race. After a spell in rather better company at Wimbledon and the departure overseas of three of the owners, it was left to Johnston to sell Kentish Kipper.

By a happy chance he found a buyer in Arthur Milton, the former Gloucestershire and England opening batsman who was a most knowledgeable supporter of greyhound racing in the West Country. Under his guidance the Kipper won race after race. Everyone was happy, though Arthur had to be persuaded not to be embarrassed by the Kipper's successes in his new ownership.

One winter's evening Brian and I were on our way to dine at the house of an eccentric friend in a remote part of Hampshire. We were still some miles short when a police car passed us. As we followed, speculation about the car's destination became near certainty until it turned into our host's drive.

We gave its two occupants time to get into the house and then followed. The interrogation was taking place in the drawing-room but stopped abruptly when Johnston threw the door open with the words, 'Quite right, officers. He's the most consummate scoundrel in the county.'

In fact, it was not our host who was involved but one of his family who had had a minor cycling accident.

Vic Lewis

It was the winter of 1970–71 and Ray Illingworth's England team had just won the Ashes – but Vic Lewis, the former band-leader, jazz musician and cricket buff, was still surprised to receive a telephone call from Brian in Australia.

Johnners had had a brainwave. He and Don Wilson, the Yorkshire and England left-arm spinner, had been doing a cabaret act to a catchy little tune called 'Show Me Your Winkle Tonight' and Brian thought it had just the lilt to emulate the England football team's World Cup victory song of a few years earlier.

With a little bit of help from Reuters' correspondent, Jon Henderson, Johnners scratched out the words and Vic was recruited to write the score and assemble the best session musicians in London to make the record. It went like this:

We've brought the Ashes back home
We've got them here in the urn
The Aussies had had them twelve years
So it was about our turn
But oh! What a tough fight
It's been in the dazzling sunlight
In spite of the boos of the mob on the Hill
We've won by two matches to nil.

When we arrived people said
The Aussies would leave us for dead
But we knew we would prove them wrong
And that's why we're singing this song
Oh! The feeling is great
For losing is something we hate
So Sydney we thank you for both of our wins
But not for those bottles and tins.

Our openers gave us a good start
And the others then all played their part
We usually made a good score
Seven times three hundred or more
The Aussies however were apt
To collapse at the drop of a hat
If they were bowled any ball that was short
It was to ten to one on they'd be caught.

In the field it was often too hot
So sometimes we felt very low
Whether rain was forecast or not
We always knew we'd have Snow
So now to go home we are free
And we're sure the Aussies agree
Though the series has been a long uphill climb
We've all had a real bumper time.

Sadly it never made it to the top of the charts and Johnners and his songsters were left to split the royalties – all of £53.86. They decided to have a draw for the money and Illy duly made it, picking out the first prize of £25 for himself and leaving Jon Henderson, John Edrich and Bob Willis to collect the consolation prizes.

J. Paul Getty

———

When I decided to build a cricket ground at Wormsley I had no idea how to arrange fixtures or arrange for eleven men in white to turn up on the appointed days. So I turned to Brian Johnston and all my problems were solved – except for that of actually winning a match.

Brian suggested teams we ought to be playing and, when they heard about it, other teams started to queue up. I made a list of cricketers present and recently retired, who had delighted me on the field, Brian put forward some names, and then produced a list of old-stagers who became such a prominent part of the first year's teams – and quite quickly the shape of a season took form.

Brian then tirelessly took on the problems of the pitch, produced a man to make covers and sight-screens and cricket was on at Wormsley.

Brian was always there to examine the wicket, check the outfield for rogue flints (a feature of the Chilterns), welcome teams and, finally, ring the bell to start play.

As long as cricket is played at Wormsley the ghost of Brian Johnston, wearing his whites and his famous co-respondent's shoes, will be seen ambling along the boundary, ice-cream cone in hand, stopping to chat to the scorers, kids playing their own games, stray dogs or distinguished guests.

Desert Island Discs

Brian Johnston's tastes in music and much more besides were reflected in his choice of eight records when he appeared on Desert Island Discs with Roy Plomley, originator of the long-running BBC programme.

1. Eton Boating Song (Eton College Music Society).
2. All the Things You Are (Hutch).
3. We'll Gather Lilacs (Vanessa Lee and Bruce Trent).
4. Double Damask (Cicely Courtneidge).
5. Strolling (Bud Flanagan).
6. Elgar's Enigma Variations (Philharmonia Orchestra conducted by Sir Malcolm Sargent).
7. Tie a Yellow Ribbon Round the Old Oak Tree (Dawn).

8. End of the Party (Barry Alexander – Brian's eldest son who took
   another name because there was already a member of Equity named
   Barry Johnston).

Brian's chosen book was John Fisher's *Funny Way to Be a Hero*, an
analysis of British music hall with detailed information about all the
great comics and comedy acts.

17

CAKES AND ALL

Brian Johnston was a man of simple pleasures when it came to eating. He liked good, old-fashioned English cooking – 'nursery or schoolboy food,' he called it – and he didn't like anyone messing about with his lunch, tea or dinner.

Nancy Doyle

Lunch at Lord's – invariably beef sandwiches on brown bread with just a pinch of salt – was served by the famous Nancy Doyle, who has presided over the best table on the county circuit for more than thirty years.

I always knew when Brian was on his way because even when I was in the kitchen I could hear him whistling as he came up the pavilion stairs.

He would come in, still whistling, say good morning, give me a kiss

Ed McLachlan

and pick up his coffee and his post, which was left here for him, and off he'd go to the commentary box.

He never changed in all the years I knew him. He was always pleasant, always in a good humour, never cross or annoyed or anything like that. And I thought he was the most wonderful man I've ever known.

Brian's wife, Pauline, is lovely, too, and though I don't know any of his children I know of them. Brian thought the world of my daughter, Janette, who was with me at Lord's as a youngster. When she got married, Brian and Pauline gave her a present and when her two children came along they gave them gifts as well. And every Christmas Brian would leave a card and a bottle of champagne for me at the back door of the pavilion.

And then there were all those cakes, loads and loads of them. He gave me one once – a beautiful cake in the shape of a cricket pitch with two batsmen, the umpires and fielders – as a gift for the Middlesex scouts who had two boys going out to a jamboree in Japan and were trying to raise some money to pay their fares. They raffled it and raised £250.

Another cake, this time in the form of a cricket bat, was raffled at Harrow Cricket Club in aid of spastic children and the woman who won it still has it in her freezer!

Brian just loved coming to Lord's – even on days when he wasn't commentating he would go up into the box to enjoy the view and do a bit of work – and I like to think he loved the dining room and the food we serve.

They tell me that the modern players are into pasta and all that stuff but they don't eat pasta with me. No way. They have a normal lunch – roast beef, filleted sirloin steak, a piece of chicken if they want it. If they want a salad, they can have a salad – but if they don't tell me before eleven o'clock they have to take what I put in front of them.

The only one I've got with a special diet – and this will surprise a few people – is Mike Gatting. People keep telling me Mike's fat because I feed him too much but all he has for lunch is a green salad, a jacket potato, a small sweet and a cup of tea. He's very good and sticks to it the whole season but, even so, he'll never be skinny because he isn't built that way.

Most of the players – England, Australia, New Zealand, the West Indies – will eat anything but you have to be a bit careful with India, Pakistan and Sri Lanka because of their religious beliefs. All they want is chicken or lamb and maybe a bit of fish.

I never had that problem with Brian. He knew exactly what he wanted – a glass of champagne and his beef sandwiches with brown bread and just a little bit of salt. Always the same – just like the man.

The last time I saw him was on 16 November 1993, when he was guest speaker at a benefit dinner for Norman Cowans in the committee dining room.

He came in to see me just beforehand and he was in such a state because he'd just found out it was a black tie dinner and he was wearing a lounge suit. He was so embarrassed it was ridiculous.

So I said to him, 'You can always blame me, you know.'

'How can I do that?' he asked.

'Well, tell them there was nothing about any dress requirement on your invitation and you rang me to ask what was the normal procedure. And I said, "Lounge suit." '

I don't know whether he did or not but I thought the best way to spare his embarrassment was to make a joke of it. And I didn't mind taking the blame. Not for Brian.

Bill Frindall

Bill Frindall kept as close an eye on the tea-time cakes in the commentary box as he did on the score.

Brian Johnston transformed the commentary box from a fairly dour and disciplined broadcasting studio to a cavern of cake and comedy. Miraculously he did this without missing a ball or interrupting the flow of play. His ability to interweave description of cricket with a well-honed music hall routine was unrivalled, a skill brilliantly exhibited during his final

Paul Russell from From Brisbane to Karachi *(Queen Anne Press)*

Test when he sandwiched into his commentary the fruits of a long joke-swapping session with Roy Hudd.

When I first joined the team, in 1966, I was forbidden to utter a word and all my statistical contributions had to be written on small cards. Brian's permanent move from the TV box four years later changed all that. It was he who endowed his colleagues with nicknames which were to echo around the world's airwaves for two decades. As 'The Bearded Wonder' (or 'Bearders'), I was installed as his stooge, a role I was only too happy to play. Now that he has gone, I know exactly how Ernie Wise must have felt when he lost the great Eric Morecambe.

Before 1970 food and drink rarely appeared in the box; afterwards they were never absent. It started when he grumbled on air after our tea had failed to appear one afternoon. Next day a lady sent a cake up to us and he thanked her during the broadcast. It did not take long for listeners to realize that 'cake' was the password for their names being mentioned. The climax came when the Egg Marketing Board sent a lady disguised as a chicken with a tray of creamy goo. Sadly, their effort went unrewarded as it coincided with Henry Blofeld's stint at the mike. Typically, he credited the Milk Marketing Board!

One day when no produce appeared, John Arlott rebuked the listeners for eating their own food and starving an OAP (Brian). He could not resist a personal plea for 'any unwanted bottles of wine'.

Rarely have I arrived at the Lord's pavilion during a Test match without a steward thrusting a cake into my already laden arms. Brian always insisted that the produce was equally distributed among broadcasters, engineers and guests, and he personally transported many cakes to children's hospitals.

When he attended my wedding two years ago, we even had to cut two cakes: the official one and another presented to Brian by a fellow guest who was a *Test Match Special* addict.

Memories of my first (televised) view of Test cricket are dominated by B.J.'s commentary, mingling the mysteries of Ramadhin's spin with our hero's ability to exact reciprocal waves from the occupants of a house whose balcony overlooked the Trent Bridge ground.

Fifteen years passed before we first met during a charity match at Ashtead where he would easily have won the noisiest fielder award ahead of Merv Hughes. A few weeks later, as the BBC's original cricket correspondent, he was a third of the panel which interviewed me in response to my application for the scoring vacancy caused by Arthur Wrigley's sudden death.

Johnners delighted in asking the most impossible questions and often pretended that he had calculated the answers himself. I even had to redesign my bowling sheet when he insisted on knowing how many boundaries each bowler had conceded.

His gaffes and leg-pulling reached a crescendo last season as a result of 'Aggers' (Jon Agnew) and 'The Doctor' (Neville Oliver) teaming up with spoof letters from 'Ivor Biggun' and 'Mrs Tess Tickle'. They even tricked him at the end-of-match presentation into announcing the name of the sponsor's chairman as 'Mr Hugh Jarce'. He exacted terrible revenge upon Aggers by arranging for the TV producer to organize a spoof interview featuring Fred Trueman and Jack Bannister on the current dearth of England fast bowlers. It is now a collector's item.

He excelled at spoonerisms and once began a Lord's Test involving Pakistan's opening bowler, Asif Masood, by revealing that 'Massive Arsood was running in from the Nursery End!' There was also that unfortunate slip when he meant to describe Henry Horton's stance as being akin to an old man sitting on a shooting stick.

In stage parlance, he was a great 'corpser' and his fits of the giggles, some lasting several minutes, caused several listeners to have road accidents or burn their ironing. His reaction to Aggers describing Botham's hit-wicket dismissal as failing to 'get his leg over', ended with him trying to finish reading the scorecard in a Michael Bentine falsetto.

News of the arrival of his first grandchild came soon after tea on the second day of the Sydney Test of January 1983 and a suitable bottle or two was broached in celebration. The notes column of my scoresheet records, 'B.J. heard his first grandson had been born an hour ago. Grandfather doing well.'

He inspired us to accept various bizarre dares, my most memorable being to score the entire day of an Ashes Test at the Oval whilst disguised as an Arab. His 'on-air' reaction to my appearance resulted in *Test Match Special* being included in *Pick of the Week* for the first time.

Johnners was so exuberant and zestful to the end that we all overlooked his age. Physically he looked in his early sixties, mentally he had never left his teens. The only reason that he had a twenty-minute break in the middle of his two-hour one-man show was to give the audience a rest. He always said he would finish after an Ashes series and would not emulate John Arlott by announcing his retirement in advance. Mercifully, someone up there was listening and ensured that he would be able to work at full bore virtually until the end. He was eighty-one years young and very, very special.

John Woodcock

John Woodcock, former cricket correspondent of The Times, *was a regular dinner companion.*

With Brian's death the game of cricket lost its best-loved friend. I really and truthfully believe that he didn't have an enemy in the world.

He himself never spoke of anyone dying. He would always refer to 'the great scorer' having called. Johnners had his own language. It was not just the *Test Match Special* team who had their nicknames. Almost all one's mutual friends did – from the 'nodder' to the 'stacker' and the 'extractor' to the 'healer'. Johnners would 'break his fast' each morning and 'take salt' at night.

He was a man of simple tastes. Dinner with him had very little to do with gastronomy. Nouvelle cuisine was to be avoided at all costs. If it was a choice between the smartest restaurant in town and the café on the corner, he would just as soon go to the latter, and he would be equally at home in either. Presented with the most extravagant menu in the world, he would have asked for smoked salmon with plenty of brown bread and butter, scrambled eggs and cold ham, and strawberry ice cream with lots of wafers, washed down, for preference, with a glass of Pouilly Fumé. Never red wine, never port, never brandy, never whisky, never anything remotely exotic.

Every match Johnners attended, every tour he went on, every conversation he joined in was the more fun for having him there. He was recorded by his mother as having laughed for the first time when he was less than a fortnight old. That, I am assured, is well ahead of schedule; but he began as he was to continue.

More than once over the years, on tours of Australia, India and elsewhere, relations between the players of cricket and the cricket Press had become somewhat strained by the time Johnners turned up. As often as not, it was because of a lack of trust between the two parties.

But into the dining room or the foyer of the hotel he would come, making that ridiculous hunting horn noise of his, which became a kind of signature tune, and saying, 'Hello, Cowders,' or 'Hello, Brearlers,' or 'Hello, Swanny,' or 'Hello, Godders,' or 'Wooders,' or 'Unders,' or 'Embers'. Suddenly the barriers would come down, and things would start to look up.

Brian had this great natural gift for fun and friendship. He was eminently, glowingly approachable. Thousands must have walked away after only the briefest of exchanges, feeling they had made not an acquaintance but a friend. Some Test cricket sides – last year's Australians, for example – took a little while to understand how the formula worked and to appreciate just how genuine Brian was. Keith Miller and Ray Lindwall, and all those of earlier generations, knew well enough; but someone like David Boon is not accustomed to being hailed as 'Booners' by relative strangers.

In South Africa on the MCC tour of 1964–65 we played Orange Free State at Bloemfontein. Brian was on the air when a certain D. Schonegeval came in to bat. 'And now,' he said, 'we have – ur – we have – um – we have "Schooners" ' – and 'Schooners' he was for evermore.

Now that the 'great scorer' has come for Johnners himself, Test match commentaries will never be quite the same again. For some they may become more usefully informative, for some less aggravatingly discursive; but they are unlikely ever again to be so consistently and unconditionally goodnatured. There will be mourning at Johnners' departing not only among cricketers, but among housewives and long-distance lorry drivers and countless others to whom, like John Arlott and Alan Gibson before him, he made the game into something more intelligible, or at any rate less arcane, than a succession of 'flippers' and 'seamers' and 'in-duckers' and 'balls not coming on to the bat.'

I knew Brian for nearly fifty years, and never, that I can remember, spent an unhappy day in his company, as distinct from an occasionally trying or disappointing one. Instinctively generous, incorrigibly corny, quite without artifice, totally loyal, unfailingly enthusiastic, highly principled, endearingly old-fashioned, surprisingly stubborn and, until he was struck down, seemingly ageless, he was a national, not to say an international, institution.

Adapted from an article in The Times.

Guards' Pudding

Not unnaturally, Brian was often asked to supply his favourite recipe for some worthwhile cause but, surprisingly, it was not for cake. His special delight was Guards' Pudding which, he always said, looked like a Christmas pudding but was delightfully light and fluffy. Here it is.

Serves 4–6

6 oz/170g fresh white breadcrumbs
6 oz/170g chopped shredded suet or butter
4 oz/115g brown or sand sugar
3 tablespoons strawberry jam
2 small eggs
1 level teaspoon bicarbonate of soda
Pinch of salt

Mix dry ingredients together. Add jam and egg beaten up with bicarbonate of soda. Mix thoroughly and then turn into a well-greased mould which should be a little more than three parts full. Steam for three hours.

For the Sauce (very important)
1 whole egg
1 egg yolk
1½ oz/45g castor sugar
2 tablespoons orange juice

Place ingredients in a bowl and then place this bowl in another bowl
of very hot water. Whisk until thick and frothy. Serve immediately
or, if not, whisk for one minute before serving.

18

APPRECIATIONS

When Brian Johnston died, countless column inches were devoted to appreciations of his life and work.

Michael Parkinson

———

From the Radio Times, *29 January 1994.*

Whereas I always imagine John Arlott among cricket's dreaming spires, I shall forever think of Brian Johnston as the amiable old buffer standing by the sight-screen with a gin and tonic in his hand. He had this affable, slightly tipsy view of the game. In his case intoxication came not from a bottle but from the realization he was being paid to do the two things in life he enjoyed most of all: talk and be in the company of cricketers.

His genius (and his contribution to radio was every bit as singular and important as anyone you care to mention) was that he made it all seem so simple. So much so that people believed that he was that most beguiling (to the English) of creatures: the gifted amateur. He was, in fact, one of the most meticulous and professional broadcasters I have ever encountered. He was, for instance, a splendid interviewer. He was clear, sympathetic and well informed. He had the gift of being interested as well as being interesting. He was an interviewer's gift. You had ten minutes to fill, wanted a laugh, four or five anecdotes, end with a boffo: Brian Johnston was your man.

As a commentator he had a wonderful gift of timing, an infallible sense of how to build tension, and the comedian's trick of relieving boredom with a laugh. He loved comedians. In many ways he was a frustrated performer who might have made a living as a front-of-cloth comic in the music halls he so adored. He was cricket's cheeky chappie. 'I say, I say, I say. The batsman's Holding, the bowler's Willey. I don't wish to know that. Kindly leave the stage.'

I was never quite sure if Brian Johnston was born with a sunny disposition or whether, like many more, he acquired it after spending five years fighting in the Second World War and deciding to make the most of what was left. He was an officer in the Grenadier Guards, fought in the campaign in north-west Europe and was awarded the Military Cross in 1945. They don't give those away, but he wouldn't talk about it. 'I was lucky,' he said. Characteristically, he called his autobiography *It's Been a Lot of Fun*.

He was born in 1912 and enjoyed a happy childhood in a beautiful Queen Anne house. His father was a prosperous City merchant. Brian went to Eton, played rugby and cricket. He read History at New College, Oxford, played cricket and had a wonderful time. On coming down he went into the family business, although his heart was in the music halls and theatres that became his favourite haunts. His love of funny men was to last a lifetime and he had some of his happiest days in broadcasting interviewing the stars he so admired.

After the war he was recruited by the outside broadcasting department of the BBC. He worked on *In Town Tonight*, reported live from theatres, the Chamber of Horrors, on stage with the Crazy Gang at the Victoria Palace. He also commentated on King George VI's funeral in 1952, the

Queen's Coronation in 1953 and a number of royal weddings. It was a thorough training in the most difficult aspects of broadcasting and it provided the foundation on which he later built his reputation for being relaxed, unflummoxed and never out of control, no matter what might happen. Ah! But what about the time he giggled helplessly in the commentary box during a Test match when Jon Agnew reported that a batsman had failed to get his leg over? Wasn't that a clear case of being out of control?

Quite the opposite. It was the best possible example of Johnston's talents as a communicator. It is a moment of wondrous intimacy such as only the best and the subtlest broadcasters can achieve. As you feel yourself engulfed in the insanity of the situation there might be just a suspicion that you have been set up. And you have, not that it matters, because you never want the madness to stop.

From 1946 to 1970 Brian Johnston presented cricket for BBC Television. Then the head of television sport decided that cricket needed a new image. So Brian Johnston moved to radio and, at an age when most men might be thinking of a pension and collecting the bus pass, embarked on the final, and in many ways, most rewarding part of an already remarkable career.

He became, with Arlott, one of the defining voices of our summer game. They were very different, both as men and as commentators. John was a poet and a connoisseur's delight, Brian was the funster who had the knack of attracting people to the game who didn't know the difference between a silly mid-on and a chocolate cake. And although the game meant many different things to both men and they had little in common, what they did agree on was that, no matter how much they enjoyed cricket, it was only a game. A full life had given them both a proper perspective of priorities, something that is sometimes missing nowadays when sporting commentary is increasingly left in the hands of those who have known no life other than that of a professional sportsman.

Brian Johnston's stint on *Down Your Way* brought out all the best qualities of the man and the broadcaster. He presented the final programme from Lord's on his 75th birthday. He had declared after 733 performances, the exact number presented by his predecessor Franklin Engelmann. As his producer Anthony Smith said: 'That was the mark of the man and his integrity.'

Brian Johnston is one of those men who makes you smile when you write about him. He was a Wodehousian figure from the tips of his two-toned shoes to the top of that remarkable head with the cab door ears and giant hooter. He looked what he was, a toff and a prankster. His humour was pretty basic. As a young man, after playing cricket for Eton Ramblers at a country house, he placed a chamber pot filled with lemonade and sausages under the bed of Colonel Cartwright, the club's secretary. He once told the nation that, 'Ray Illingworth has just relieved himself at the Pavilion End.' Or what about: 'It's close of play here, but they go on till seven o'clock at Edgbaston. So over now for some more balls from Rex Alston.'

Reporting on Peter Pollock, the South African fast bowler, spraining an ankle, he said: 'Bad luck on Peter. He's obviously in great pain. It is especially bad luck as he is here on honeymoon with his pretty young wife. Still he'll probably be all right tomorrow if he sticks it up tonight.'

When New Zealand's Glenn Turner was hit on the box with the fifth ball of an over Johnston told us: 'It looks as if he is going to try and continue. He still looks very shaken and pale. Very plucky of him. Yes, he's definitely going to have a try – one ball left.'

Whenever we remember Brian Johnston in the future, and he will be remembered so long as the game is played, we will recall the joy and laughter that suffused the man. What pleased Brian most of all was that, 21 years after being retired from the BBC, he was still working. When he suffered his heart attack at the age of 81 he was on the way to an engagement and had a full diary. His triumph was that he had reached the ninth decade of his life and had never grown old.

Tim Rice

From the Daily Telegraph, *6 January 1994.*

Brian Johnston has been part of my life for as long as I can remember, from the time of his column for the young readers of the *Eagle* in the fifties, through *In Town Tonight* in the pioneering days of cricket on television, through commentaries on occasions both State and trivial, through radio quiz-shows both witty and daft, through *Down Your Way* and, above all, through *Test Match Special.*

Somewhere along the line the fan became a friend but it's impossible to pinpoint when; all Johnners fans were friends too, whether they were lucky enough to know him personally, or whether they only knew his ebullience and youthful warmth from the airwaves.

The man behind the microphone was the man himself – this has already been said so many times in tribute since the sad news yesterday morning, for it is this aspect of Brian that first and foremost springs to mind.

It was as if he were commentating on the wonderful things around him for every waking hour – at times there happened to be a microphone there, at times there wasn't, but this made no difference to his delight in observing and communicating his enthusiasms. And as far as Brian was concerned, wonderful things were always in the ascendant – he was the antithesis of the media legions for whom good news is no news.

This is truly the end of an era. The hackneyed old phrase is for once accurate, is for once entirely appropriate. Although Brian himself was always the first to acknowledge that it was superb team-work that made *Test Match Special* such a triumph, it will never be the same animal.

No-one could become the next Johnners, just as no-one could have become another John Arlott, a broadcaster whose genius Johnners indisputably matched.

I have only once in my life had to pull my car on to the hard shoulder as a result of excessive laughter threatening to make me a danger to fellow motorists. This was as a result of Brian's epic 'Botham leg-over' *contretemps* with Jon Agnew in 1991.

To listen to Johnners manfully struggle his way through the score-card despite a serious attack of hysterics was to hear the supreme professional, the supreme entertainer and the supreme good egg all on simultaneously immaculate form.

One hundred years from now the humour of that moment will shine as brightly as ever, as will so many other Johnston highlights, light-hearted and serious.

He kept going at full tilt to the very end. There is tiny consolation in the fact that his last series, in which he sparkled as irresistibly as ever, was against the old enemy, Australia, and that his final Test match was a long-awaited England victory.

His knowledge of cricket and its history was great, and his support for England always crystal clear, without in any way hampering his respect for those opponents who defeated us. Neither would he criticise the modern player for being a modern player. He was a traditional-ist but he moved with the times.

He and Pauline must have derived great pleasure from the fact that they established their own cricket tradition by means of the party they gave after the Friday of every Lord's Test match.

There have been few more enjoyable events in any sporting calendar as the Johnstons in their home repeating the formula of seemingly effortless hospitality and enthusiasm that graced all Brian's broadcasting. His family are yet another tribute to him.

In addition to the prodigious workload of broadcasting and personal appearances, Brian attended, usually in a star capacity, a huge number of cricketing and charitable functions at home and abroad. At those he had the knack of making every fellow guest, chum or stranger, feel that he was particularly welcome, which as far as Brian was con-cerned, he almost always was.

Johnners saw the best in the worst of us, and thus encouraged the very best in all of us.

Brian Johnston simply proved that the old-fashioned values of good manners, professionalism and optimism could still work in the most cynical and rushed of times. From his distinguished war service to the most ephemeral wireless encounter, he put everything he had into everything he did.

He will be missed by millions of friends and admirers because it was impossible for any of them to be one without being the other.

Marmaduke Hussey

The Chairman of the Board of Governors of the BBC remembers 'a fine and lovely man in every way.'

Brian Johnston inspired affection and admiration in full measure wherever he went, and the countless tributes have borne witness to that. He was a man of many gifts: courage, humour, eloquence, charm, a total lack of side, and an unrivalled ability to make friends with anyone at any time or place. He had no enemies, and I doubt whether he had any critics either. He was the essence of good humour.

He also had an encyclopaedic knowledge of many sports, but particularly of course cricket, matched by a keen eye for detail, the incongruous and the unexpected. His unique broadcasting talent, first on radio, then on television, and finally and triumphantly on *Test Match Special*, made him a national figure and a much-loved one.

But beneath that easy bonhomie was a man of deep feeling and serious intent. His great love for Pauline and his family, his constant and devoted work for charity, and his instinctive sympathy for those less fortunate demonstrated a sincere and genuine understanding and compassion that was as much a part of his character as his hilarious speeches and comic turns.

And he was a true and steadfast friend. At an awkward moment, one look from Brian, not even a word, was enough to signify sympathetic support and enough to strengthen one's determination. He was always like that, throughout his life: a great character to have around when the going was tough, difficult or dangerous – calm, confident and resolute in awkward circumstances; charming, funny and buoyant in happier ones. A fine and lovely man in every way.

Mike Howell

Mike Howell, a blind cricket-lover from Oldham, was one of Brian's special friends.

Life's tape rewinds a rapid thirty years to a warm July: that it was the beginning of a long college summer holiday raised the spirits by dint of freedom alone; that VIP guest tickets had been obtained for the five days of an Old Trafford Test match was a rich treat in store; that, thanks to our letters and his personal radio messages to me three weeks earlier, I would meet and hopefully record a few conversations with Australian commentator Alan McGilvray was good fortune virtually beyond a young man's belief.

Yet there was a nagging challenge involved. When a youngster leaves home unaccompanied for the first time and returns safely, there is reason to rejoice at the accomplishment of independence. That milestone comes later for a young blind person (who needs orientation training), but the attainment is of greater significance to both parents and offspring. While my mother was willing to take me to the ground and bring me back each evening, my father favoured use of the five days as an important mobility exercise for me. I set out on the first day in secret apprehension, though of quite what I am no longer sure. As the paternal challenge was met and the maternal worries subsided, aided by the friendly helpfulness of people encountered en route, so too did I feel totally at ease by the fourth day.

After having made a recording with, and been well lagered by, Alan McGilvray during the fourth day, I resumed my seat in the Board of

Control Stand and became aware of familiar voices in front of me. Should I turn the tape recorder on or not? . . . *Got them!*

'He's not going to give it away today, thank goodness.' That obviously meant Ted Dexter who'd survived for three hours without attempting to take control of the game.

'He'll really let go soon, though,' and there was immediate laughter from the two friends following sudden characteristic Dexter violence.

'Oh, what a beauty!' Lifted by this moment in England's hearty fight-back, I moved forward and declared their names as if making a triumphant arrest.

'Mr Brian Johnston and Mr Denis Compton.' For just a jittery moment I had no idea what would happen and contemplated sitting down in the instant it took Brian to turn and look right at me.

'Hello there,' greeted an astonishingly deep voice at close range. 'Denis, you must meet my young friend who was introduced to me by Peter West,' mistook or invented Brian as if we were on air. We laughed about this introduction in later years, but I introduced myself by name and as an interloper.

'I heard what you were saying about Ted and couldn't resist telling you that at the nets this morning he was deadly serious about today. "Pitch 'em up," he kept insisting louder and *louder – "pitch 'em up!"*

'There you are, Compers, I told you – he's earnest today as well as Ted.'

'I'll bet you, Brian, he's not there at the close. I'd very much like him to be but he'll cut loose soon.'

' "Pitch em up",' imitated Brian in reminder of the Dexter resolve, followed by another cannon-cracker which brought the crowd to life and Brian to appreciative commentary.

'Would you have swept on this pitch, Denis?' I asked.

'Swept!' chipped in Brian, 'he'd have had the broom out to them every over! Anyway, we'd better get back up and tell Peter West you're here,' he teased, before a final considerate enquiry as to whether I'd be all right at the close of play. 'You must be very brave to come here all on your own,' he congratulated me warmly as we shook hands. Such golden memories could hardly be sweetened by the elapse of time.

The friendship was firmly established by the time the Peter West fabrication was put to rights five years later when I was hemmed in the midst of a gaggle of tea-sipping commentators on a cool, damp June morning. While verdicts were being passed and plaudits sought among the mutual admiration society, Brian introduced me to Jim Swanton.

'Where's he from?' was the booming demand with accompanying handshake.

'Ask him,' advised Brian liltingly.

'Oldham,' I put in to spare indignity to the doyen.

'They play the *other* game there, don't they?'

'Yes, but let's not talk about that – let's talk about Sobers instead.'

'Have you ever met him?' asked Jim with interest.

'Yes, my brothers and I *actually* had a twenty-minute private audience with the great man after a match which he came to play in Saddleworth in 1961. He was terrific with us – they shut everybody else out of the pavilion.'

'What did you ask him about?' posed Brian. I laughed at the memory.

'There was no cricket chat for the first five minutes because when I declined his offer of a cigarette and told him I only smoked at college, he thought this was very curious and asked a lot of intrigued questions about under-age smoking and beer-drinking.'

'You couldn't have had a better player offer you a Player,' interjected Brian.

'They get *worse* with every season, Brian,' castigated Jim richly. 'And what had he done in the match?' asked Jim.

'He took six wickets and hit nine sixes into the river at the far end of the ground.'

'They must have got pretty fed up with that,' conjectured Jim.

'Who?' queried Brian, 'the fielders or the fishing authorities!'

How gratifying it all was, particularly in the early years, to know that Brian was happy to spend so much time with me when he was not broadcasting. The mutually unashamed elements of the eternal schoolboy were often evident in our discussions and wheezes.

'Why weren't you here when I came down earlier this morning?' demanded Brian playfully on the second morning of the 1987 Old Trafford Test against Pakistan.

'Urgent business, sir,' I explained with a quiver. 'I put five hundred pounds on this match being a draw.' It was almost worth the brief investment for the thrill of causing Brian's sudden alarm.

'You might lose your money,' he spluttered in panic.

'No, no,' I assured before talking him through the logic of my 'poor weather outlook' move. The revelation went out in his next broadcast and the *Manchester Evening News* ran a (with photograph) feature on Brian, myself and the bet. I 'collected' the following Wednesday, but Manchester bookmakers are perhaps bad losers as they would not accept future challenges once a Test match had started.

Though most of my cricket spectating has been at Old Trafford, adventures to other venues give equal pleasure. When last attending a Headingley Test, Brian sent me a 'Look forward to seeing you' letter and a postcard for the gateman. It didn't begin 'Dear Gaters,' but it did say: 'This is to introduce a very dear friend of mine, and it would be a great kindness to me if you could bring him to the football stand and let him sit in one of our seats below the commentary box. I shall come and thank you personally before the end of the match.'

When I expressed thanks for the 'ticket', Brian summed up shrewdly: 'They all know me, of course, and they see your problem immediately. Anyway, no-one would have paid money willingly to watch England today – they were *dreadful* – but I'm glad you came to see me.'

Another letter arrived a few months later in the dead of winter.

'I shall be in your area on Monday, 9 February to give one of my talks in the evening. I should very much like to take you out to lunch on that day, as I hear you're a big eater, and hope this gives you enough notice.

'If the weather's likely to be bad, I may come by train, so you'd better let me know how much it costs to 'old 'em on a bus these days.'

The occasion was at least as good as the prospect. When comfortably in the warmth of a well-populated town centre restaurant, the conversation level gradually dipped to a low hum as we ordered and continued our animated discussion. Then the patrons, not backward in coming forward once the first had made the move, came to our table either in quest of Brian's autograph or to greet me. The score was 11–6 to Brian when I realized that he had finished his main course with half my sixteen-ounce steak still remaining.

'Keep eating, for goodness sake,' urged Brian as the place began to empty. 'Radio 3 are coming over to us in ten seconds and Chris Martin-Jenkins is covering for BBC2.' To the mirth of management and my near indigestion, a pulsating commentary was given, including striking rate, the meat meter readings and the chip count, until the final applauded mouthful.

When the telephone rang at around what would normally have been teatime, a lugubrious voice asked:

'Would you be available for a four-course dinner with us this evening?'

'Not if there's to be another of your commentaries, thanks, Brian.'

'I've been talking to the chap who's running this thing tonight and he says he knows you. If you can come, he'll pick you up in twenty minutes.'

Another cracking good meal was followed by a sparklingly brilliant Brian Johnston entertainment whose content, fluency and timing had the polish of a meticulously edited broadcast.

With the vital Johnston attribute of public popularity, 'magical Margaret', my wife, could have advised the Manchester–Oldham fare authoritatively as she has driven buses in the area since 1978. When Brian heard the details of our delightfully fatalistic meeting, he caused David Lloyd's apprehension when next on air.

'Would you like to hear a really romantic story, David?'

'Oh no, Johnners! – what's coming now?'

'No, no, this is utterly true and absolutely wonderful.' So it was and so it is, with a resultant press article, magazine feature and our commentary box presence the following day in time to meet Mike Hendrick before he took his 'Call the Commentators' seat.

'Our next caller,' announced Brian at one point, 'is Mrs Spencer of Southampton. How's the weather with you today, Mrs Spencer?'

'Just at the moment it's absolutely pi-- pouring down with rain. I was out in the garden bowling to my husband a few minutes ago but we had to come in.'

'Nice to know you still have a few balls out there every now and then. Anyway, what's your question?'

Margaret grabbed my arm urgently.

'Brian's just written in the condensation on the window "Baxter is a twerp",' she whispered with restrained laughter. 'I don't think Peter's going to do anything till they've finished, but isn't it like being back at school again?'

As a cricket-lover with a sound sense of practicalities, it was admirable that Margaret should have wanted us to attend the 1993 Benson and Hedges Final but, at kindest expression, 'a woman's prerogative' to make known her wish when all tickets had probably been sold.

'I'd really love to watch Lancashire in a final at Lord's and see Brian and Chris again,' she coaxed meaningfully. Thwarted locally in eleventh-hour attempts to oblige the challenge, I eventually telephoned Brian with unprecedented reluctance.

'Of course I won't buy tickets on your behalf,' he told me firmly. 'You're friends of mine, so I'd give them to you as a gift if you can come. They'll be waiting for you at the Grace Gates.'

The abundant detail of that monumental day's adventure is highlighted by the (again unsweetened) memories of Lancashire's fumbles, their later heroic fight and final failure in the dark; Margaret's elated comment that Brian's eyes had sparkled on presentation of the goodies we'd brought him and the wholesome prospect of more of my mother's professional cuisine; Brian's tolerance of the pushes, interruptions and shouts of adulation as we made our slow way from the ground; and Margaret's pitching merrily into Stilton and port on our 2.30 a.m. return without sign of fatigue from the last twenty-two hours and the 400-mile drive.

From these personal reminiscences and the rich treasury of our price-less private recordings spanning over twenty-five years, it is fitting that the self-deprecation of Brian's 'Someone Who Was' is elevated to the deserved citation 'Someone Who Won'.

19

CLOSE OF PLAY

Jack Sokell

The coal-mining villages of South Yorkshire are a long way from Eton, Oxford, the Guards and the BBC, so it tells you much about Brian Johnston that he was held in as much affection there as he was anywhere else.

Jack Sokell is secretary of the Wombwell Cricket Lovers' Society which is to establish a Brian Johnston Memorial Coaching Scholarship which will send one of its youngsters each year for special coaching under the former MCC coach, Don Wilson, at Ampleforth College.

We at Wombwell have many happy memories of Brian ever since our then patron, the late Denzil Batchelor, persuaded him to come to a meeting at our Horse Shoe Hotel headquarters shortly after our formation in 1951.

He came on a cricket panel with Ken Grieves and Frank Tyson and was in great form with the two cricketers as fascinated as the rest of us by his humour and love of the game. That visit resulted in close links with our society and he was always interested in our progress and activities, especially our work for young cricketers.

Brian always stayed with our then president, Dr Leslie Taylor, and his late wife, Mollie, who was a sister of the much-loved former Yorkshire and England cricketer, Roy Kilner, who died at an early age in 1928. Brian was able to talk with Mollie about Roy, whose funeral drew a huge crowd estimated at around 100,000 to Wombwell, and delve through the memorabilia of his career.

He also developed a close link with the Taylors' gardener and often their conversations would result in Brian having to make a rapid car dash to Doncaster to catch a later train back to London.

Another treasured memory is of Brian joining us on the Sunday of a Headingley Test for a match to celebrate the Queen's Silver Jubilee. Christopher Martin-Jenkins and Michael Parkinson captained the respective teams of sporting stars and stage and TV personalities and Brian was in his element, strolling around the ground, talking to the spectators and paying regular visits to the tea room for apple pie and fresh cream. The locals still remember his friendliness and his common touch.

In 1993 the Society introduced our new Jack Fingleton Memorial Award for the cricket commentator of the year and Brian was elected the first winner. On hearing the news, he wrote back, 'I am delighted and chuffed to be the first winner of an award to the memory of a dear friend.'

Alas, we will not be able to present his award during the 1994 Headingley Test as we had intended but we feel that Brian would have been equally chuffed by our decision to introduce the Brian Johnston Memorial Coaching Scholarship which will be linked to our coaching classes in addition to our Sir Jack Hobbs and John Arlott scholarships.

Over the years, Brian was a regular contributor to our world-famous annual 12th Man magazine and he cemented a close friendship with our cricket poet, the late Les Bailey, who supplied him with many examples of his work.

Naturally, when we paid tribute to Brian with a dinner on his receipt of our Denzil Batchelor Memorial Award for services to English cricket, Les produced the ideal verses for this lovable man.

A life full of moment, bonhomie and cheer
From Eton to Oxford to a young Grenadier,
BBC Outside Broadcasts and pastures quite new
Where he even survived being once sawn in two.
Now a rich sense of humour, an eloquent style
Has added to cricket a reason to smile.
And all the world over where the great game is played
The sunshine of commentary is the memory he made.
At cricket, Monte Carlo or just Down Your Way
We'll remember him always – till the last close of play.

Tony Hart